Tiger's Adventures *in the* Everglades

VOLUME THREE

As told by T. F. Gato

jay gee heath

Copyright © 2019
All rights reserved. No part of this book may be reproduced, scanned, or transmitted in any form or by any means, electronic or mechanical, including photocopying, recording, or by any information storage and retrieval system, without permission from the copyright owner.
All characters appearing in this work are fictitious. Any resemblance to real persons, living or dead, is purely coincidental. Names, characters, places, and incidents either are the product of the author's imagination or are used fictitiously, and any resemblance to any actual persons, living or dead, events, or locales is entirely coincidental.

ISBN: eBook 13: 978-0-9890712-7-7
ISBN Print Book 13: 978-0-9890712-6-0

Library of Congress Control Number: 2017912570

Publisher
Joyce G Heath, Naples, Fl

ALSO BY JAY GEE HEATH

Right Talents
Right Skills
Right Dreams
Right Response
Right Target
Tiger's Adventures in the Everglades
Tiger's Adventures in the Everglades Volume Two

DEDICATION

To Sam

Always encouraging

ACKNOWLEDGEMENT

Thanks to both my sisters and my neighbor for their help and inspiration

Janet Benjamins
Jo Anne Sullivan
Jean Smith

Art by K. T. Gato

As we can all see from the pictures, Tiger is not a Maine Coon cat.
Tiger's Adventures predate Hurricane Irma when Flamingo was a different place. During his adventures, the Park Service ran the campground operations which have since been turned over to the concessionaire.

TABLE OF CONTENTS

The Three Turkeys 1
Big Birds 29
Take Your Cat to Work Day 49
Truck Boat Crash 71
Black Olives 91

Rae's Recipes 109

LIST OF ILLUSTRATIONS

1. Reddish Egret 1
2. Reddish Egret 2
3. Tiger and Turkey
4. Buzzards Flying
5. Sluggo Barking
6. Sluggo Howling
7. Tiger Snarling
8. Lizard
9. Ghost Orchid
10. Skimmer
11. Heron with Fish
12. Tiger and Crow
13. Tiger with Rat Shoe
14. Tiger with Pizza

THREE TURKEYS

She was hopping mad. Really. Hopping mad. Though hopping is too mild a term. Makes me think about little rabbits or grasshoppers, and playtime. No, not hopping. More like. Raging. Boiling. Boiling mad. Yeah. Really boiling mad. Furious, seething, stamping foot mad. Not sure I've ever seen her quite this angry. Not even when I used her black velvet dress for a pillow. And that was an accident. Well, mostly an accident. I did go in the closet and sleep on her dress, but only because it was on the floor. It kind of got stuck on my claw and slid off the hanger and fell, and it was soft and warm, and smelled a little of her. I hadn't meant to leave cat fur on the velvet, but the fabric just sort of grabbed it and hung on. I never meant to make her mad. Never mad. I always aim for just on the border of amazed wonder with a side of exasperation under a hidden smile. I wouldn't want her this mad at me.

But now? Man. Something sure has set her off. I edge to the doorway, keeping my tail close. Kevlar isn't trying to calm her. He's listening. From a few steps away. She's yelling in her really quiet voice. The one that means she's reached her limit. When she uses that tone on me, I do whatever she says. I don't even ask how high, just jump, and hope I get it right.

I stay in the doorway, ready to turn and run.

Maybe she found what I did. I don't hear my name. Besides, it was an accident, it wouldn't make her mad, just kind of annoyed with a sprinkle of pride.

She stomps her foot again. Kevlar backs up a step.

Huh. Smart man. I've never seen her this angry. I really hope it's not the toy rabbit. It's not the velvet dress, she already found that.

"Catfish. Who does he think he is?" She spits out the words.

Not me. Not the bunny. Catfish. Something Catfish did.

"He can't do this to me. I'm only supposed to work a half day. But his turdface buddy decides he wants the day off. This morning he decides he wants today off." She waves a hand at Kevlar. "And I have to fill in." She stomps her foot, again. "This morning," she repeats with her teeth together.

Her tone raises my hackles and I think I see Kevlar's neck hairs sticking up.

She is wired.

"Catfish tells me to work, decides I can fill in. At the last minute. Today of all days." She raises her hands to shoulder level and shakes them once.

"Arghh." She takes a deep breath and looks at Kevlar. Winding down, I think.

"What am I going to do, Kev? I can't work and cook for the chickee. What am I going to do?" Not quite a wail, more pleading.

Feeling encouraged, I step into the room, but keep my distance. Not too close, don't want my tail anywhere near her feet if she goes stomping.

Kevlar reaches out and pulls her into him, wrapping his arms around her. She lets him, so he timed it right. She hides her head in his shoulder and he rubs her back up and down.

I don't like people to rub my back fur the wrong way. But it works for Boston.

And he's smart enough not to say, there, there, which would probably make her hit him. He doesn't say anything. Just waits. Holding in a smile.

She was pretty funny. Stomping around.

She can't see his smile.

She finally backs away a bit calmer. "I can't do anything. He says work, I work. I have no choice. Makes me so mad. Want to slap him." She takes another deep breath and starts pacing.

I move close to the chair. My tail carefully tucked underneath.

She's thinking now. "Though I do get to say when I take breaks." Planning. Plotting. Catfish better watch out because payback is the pits.

"I can quit," she says. "Right. I know. I know. Not

happening. I'm not going to quit. Probably what he's hoping. But there's no one else to manage the campground, and Thanksgiving's always a busy day."

She walks around the room, pacing, not stomping. Kevlar and I watch. He cocks an eyebrow at her and she almost smiles. She really has cooled off. She walks to him and kisses him on the cheek. "Thanks for letting me vent. I shouldn't let him make me crazy like that."

"Good. You were pretty steamed, stomping. Don't think I ever saw you do that before," he said, adding a smile. "Kind of cute."

She gives him a fake punch in the arm.

"I have to figure out how to fix this." She checks her watch. Looks at me, thoughtfully.

What me? Why? Did she find the bunny?

No, she's not looking at me. She's thinking.

"I can get some things done before I go in. Maybe split my lunch hour. But that's still not going to cut it."

Rachel walks in, stretching. Boston's sister. Visiting for the holiday. We all look at her.

She stops short. Freezes. Catlike, though she doesn't know anything about cats.

"What?" Her eyes go back and forth between the two of them. "What did I do? I didn't do anything," she says nervously, still not moving.

Did she break something too? That's the way I act when I'm guilty and get caught.

"I'm not up too early, am I?" She moves, but only

enough to check behind her, hoping we are all looking at something back there.

"Why are you looking at me like that?" She takes a step back. "I didn't break any rules. I only killed two mosquitoes. You said I could kill mosquitoes. And no one saw me do it."

That's my standard excuse. Maybe she does know about cats.

She glances down at me. "I didn't hurt your cat. She glowered at me and blocked the doorway. I sort of flicked her back with my foot. I never even touched her. Honest."

"Him, Rae, not her," Boston says.

Rae looks back and forth with a fake smile. "I don't care what she told you, I didn't touch her. You know how intimidating she can be. She frightens Mom all the time, Boston."

Yep. Their mom is fun to torment, easy. Not a challenge like Rachel.

Kevlar keeps a straight face. Boston snorts. "He. Him. It's a boy cat. Argh. You got me using the wrong pronouns now. **He** is a boy cat and **he** didn't tell us anything. You're telling tales on yourself. Don't kick my cat."

"I didn't kick her, him. I told you. I nudged him."

"Okay. Okay. I'll talk to him. He shouldn't be threatening you."

Wasn't threatening. Just sitting in the doorway. I think Rae's afraid of cats. Of Maine Coon cats anyhow. I'm not quite a Maine Coon, but I have the size and temperament. And I'm a good hunter. Besides, I was in the doorway first.

I find a spot to clean on my chest.

"Give him a treat, Rae. He'll decide he likes you," Boston tells her.

I look up at that. *Treat?* I'm not that easy. Well, I may be. Depends on the treat. And how many.

Boston takes a breath. "Rae, I need a favor. A big favor. The whole party tonight depends on you now."

Rachel asks, "What do you mean? Do you mean the Thanksgiving dinner at that chickee place?"

"Yes, the chickee."

"How can the chickee party depend on me? You told me it's a potluck and everyone brings something. You have a signup sheet." She giggles. "And you check it twice a day."

"Yes, everyone brings something. But they're guys, Rae. The seasonals bring a six-pack and a bag of chips. I'm doing the main course and some side dishes," Boston says patiently.

Rae looks from Boston to Kevlar. "It's at the chickee, right. Not here. I don't have to clean, do I? I mean, the building is just a screened in terrace with a cement floor. I guess I could sweep. Is that what you mean?" She dips her head, worried.

"You don't have to clean. We swept it out a few days ago. Later, you could put the tablecloths on the picnic tables. That's not the problem," Boston says.

Rae frowns. "Oohh, I'm not going to like this, am I?"

"I have to work. My boss just called me in. I need

your help. If I'm working in the campground, I can't be home cooking."

"No kidding, so?" She waits, but no one says anything.

Even I can see where this is going.

"You're not thinking I'm going to cook, are you? Cook what?" she asks suspiciously.

"Three turkeys and, um, a cake?"

Three turkeys? I love turkey. Does three mean I get one?

"Turkeys? You want me to cook a turkey. No. Three turkeys?"

Boston nods her head.

"No way. Remember the famous line? *I don't know nothing about cooking no turkeys.*"

"I'll walk you through it. Come on. It will be an adventure Rae," Boston wheedles.

"I've never even cooked one turkey, forget about three."

"Three are no harder than one. If you can cook one, you can cook three. I'm signed up for three. And it's not Thanksgiving without turkey. Come on Rae. You're a really good cook. You can do it."

Rae considers that. "So. Maybe." She draws that out. "Okay. If you promise to walk me through it. And you'll owe me."

Boston hugs her. "Great. You are a life saver."

"How do you propose to walk me through the steps when you're in the campground and I'm here?"

"Easy. That's what cell phones and the internet are for. Besides. You put the turkeys in the oven and just baste them once in a while."

"You'll show me?"

"Yes. I made one cake last night, the chocolate pistachio Bundt cake. I thought the second would be chocolate strawberry. We can start it together and stuff the turkeys."

"What does that mean? Stuff. I have to do stuffing?" She's panicking now.

"The stuffing's all made. I did it last night, but we have to put it in the turkeys."

"Can't we just cook it in a pan?"

"No. Inside the turkey. Better flavor. Anything that doesn't fit in the turkeys, can bake in a pan."

Rae looks around the room.

"I boiled the giblets last night too, so you don't have to cook them."

"Giblets? For stuffing?"

"For giblet gravy."

"Gravy. I'm going to make gravy?" She gasps in horror taking a step back. "Giblet gravy?"

"No. Kev will make the gravy when he gets off duty. He'll make a roux and add the cut-up giblets. Will you cut up the giblets?" Boston asks her tentatively.

"I suppose," she says and then laughs. "I rue the day I decided to come visit."

Boston laughs too. "Rachel. It will be fun. I'll split my lunch hour and come by and help. Instead of just hanging around watching me cook today, you get to be a hero. Tiger will help."

"You should lock her up."

Lock me up?

"Him. Him."

"Okay. You should lock him in the bedroom. Protect us both."

"He doesn't like being locked up. He'd holler and scratch at the door and drive you crazy." She turns to me. "You want to help, don't you Tiger."

If I get food.

Kevlar adds encouragement. "You'll be dining out on this story for years, Rae."

Rae sniffs. "As if. What about beans? Or peas? Shouldn't I be doing those too?" she asks sarcastically.

"Yes. Good thing you mentioned it. I almost forgot, there's a three gallon can of beans in the closet, though I should be able to do those at the last minute after work. You can start them if you want."

Rae slaps herself on the forehead. "Teach me to keep my mouth shut."

"You're a good sister Rae, and I'll owe you. If you didn't help, we'd all be eating potato chips and dip. No turkey. Thanks."

"Do I get to pick my payment," Rae asks. "Because I've always been fond of your velvet dress."

"I'll tell you a story about that dress later," Boston says looking at me. She hugs Rae, checks her watch, and pulls out some bowls. "Let's start that cake. And peel the turkeys."

"Peel turkeys? How do you peel a turkey?"

"No. I meant, take the wrapping off. Let's get the cake

going first." They walk into the kitchen and I follow. She did say turkey.

Kevlar heads out to work. "I'll check in but call if you need me. Either one of you."

"Will do."

I get comfortable on a chair and nap while they mix the cake. One ear listening for the magic snack word.

"Okay. Cake should be done in forty-five minutes," Boston says as she sticks it in the oven. "Let me show you how to stuff this turkey. Then you can do the other two in the chickee. The oven down there is enormous, lots bigger than mine. Here, the turkey wrappings have instructions on them if you forget. First, put the bird in the sink because it will drip over everything." She gets down a large saucer and pours the drippings from the wrapper into it and puts it on the floor.

"Here Tiger, come get some turkey juices."

I don't move.

"Come on Tiger. Turkey juices. You love turkey."

I do. But she has to beg.

"Come on kitty. Come sniff."

"If she doesn't want it, why don't you just throw it away?" Rachel asks.

What? I look at her in shock.

"He, Rach. He. He's a cat. He can't just come over and eat. He wants me to persuade him. Watch. Good kitty."

Hmm. Smells good. I jump to the floor and sit. She moves the bowl in front of me. I look up at her and then down into the bowl. Lower my head a fraction and take a taste. Then lap it all up slowly. Turkey is my favorite.

"Do you always feed her, um, him like that?"

"Sometimes. He can get fussy. But he keeps me company and it makes us both happy. You try it when I'm gone. He's good to talk to."

Rae looks doubtful.

Boston points out the giblets and asks tentatively. "Can you chop the liver? Can you pick the neck bones, too? No pressure. I can do it when I get off work."

Liver? I perk up my ears. I love liver. I love giblets.

Rae gives her the evil eye. "I guess. Chop the liver, pick the neck bone."

"Good. You're a good sport. Tiger can have a few small pieces. You can make friends. No bones."

Yes! Turkey.

Boston's moves over to the sink and shows Rae how to rinse the turkey and stuff it. "Do the same with the other two, and pop them in the oven at, um," she looks at her watch, "eleven. Now, I have to get out of here. Call if you need me or just want to talk. Check the cake with a toothpick for doneness in forty minutes. You know how to bake a cake. Thanksgiving would be a disaster without turkey. Probably what my boss is hoping."

"He's a creep."

"You're right," Boston says and goes out the door.

"Well. I'm the chief cook." Rae looks around the kitchen. Nods her head. Looks at me. "We're in this together kid."

Not so sure about that.

"Might as well chop the giblets while the cake is cooking. Tiger, there might be a small piece for you."

Together. Yes. We're in this together. I jump up on a stool. To be close.

She talks as she chops. "I lived with a cat; you know."

Is she joking?

"Sasha, a white angora with blue eyes. Deaf. My vet said my lifestyle wasn't good for a deaf cat. I gave her up to a family familiar with the care and protection of a deaf cat. I cried. I wasn't sure if it was the right thing to do, but I have visitation rights and Sasha is happy where she is."

How do you know that?

"When I visit, she comes to sniff and say hi and then curls up in her lady's lap."

Okay.

Rae tears a strip of meat off the neck bone and passes it down to me.

I like Rae.

Rae talks as she works, like we're sitting over coffee. Almost like Boston. I guess they really are sisters.

She hands me a piece of liver.

I love liver.

"You know, we have time, I think I'll make another cake. And my special onions. If Boston has carrots, I might cook those up too."

Yuk. Veggies. I wander over to look at the torn bunny. But it's boring, so I push Boston's toy under the chair and nap while Rae works. And talks. To me? She doesn't seem to care if I listen.

She walks to the chickee twice, to stuff those turkeys and then to baste them. I let her go by herself and check the counters to see if she left out anything for me.

Nothing. Maybe I don't like her.

She wakes me later. "Want to help at the chickee?" she asks.

Huh? I raise my head.

"I know you go out with Boston."

Well, yeah, I could go.

"You better not run away. If you're good, I'll give you turkey back at the house."

Oh. Okay, I don't know about good, but I'm not running away.

It's a quick walk across the grass. She's carrying a big pan of the extra stuffing which I hope she doesn't drop. Hope she does.

She doesn't. With a groan she puts the pan on the counter. "Wow. That was heavy, but it didn't fit in the oven in the house." She drops a few pieces on the floor and I almost eat a small piece of celery. Doesn't smell tasty and I leave it and the onions, but get all the bread; then wander around the chickee while she works. And talks.

Nothing here. Not even any new mouse or rat smells. I find a little frog and chase him, but he hides behind a table leg and I can't reach him.

"All done," Rae says. "Turkeys are looking good, I guess. Let's go home and get a cup of tea. For me. Snack for you."

Liver?

Squawking noises distract us. "What in the world is that racket?"

We both look toward the sound down by the shoreline where a reddish egret is fishing.

"What's wrong with that bird?" she asks.

Nothing really. I know all about them. He's a long-legged wading bird. This one is hopping around like the crazy bird he is. His neck and head are a kind of a copper color, not red. The rest of him is gray. But still, they call him reddish. He squawks, jumps in the air, wings flapping. Then runs left. Runs right. To the left again. Sometimes leads with his head, his body following, other times leading with his body and his head trailing behind. Now he leads with the middle of his neck with both wings raised, both legs bowed out.

"I'm getting pictures of this. Boston won't believe me otherwise."

The bird runs in a circle. Hops on one foot. Raises a wing. Then raises both. Reddish egrets have a lot of energy.

"Wow, that bird got into some real good loco weed." Rae fiddles with her cell phone.

He leaps in the air again. Fluffs out his feathers, dances a few steps, raises both wings and runs along the shoreline chasing something in the water.

Rae's kind of dancing like the bird, mimicking his antics. I don't know which one to watch.

The bird stabs down in the water and comes up with a fish, flips it, swallows it.

"Huh. I don't believe it. He ate it. He ate that fish. Look. Wait until I tell Boston. Wow. Wait until I show Boston the video."

She heads for the shore but startles the bird. It screams and flies off.

"Aw. I wanted closeups." She shrugs and turns back to the house. "Oh, well, home and tea."

And liver.

She gives me a piece of liver while her tea is boiling. Yea.

"I saw what you did."

What? Is she talking to me? I look at her with narrowed eyes. She was the one jumping up and down.

"In the living room. Behind the chair." She nods toward where the toy is hidden.

Not me.

"Boston liked that stuffed animal."

I didn't do it. It tore when I shook it. The fuzzy tail just sort of came off. Besides no one saw me do it.

"I can fix it. Mend it. She'll never know."

I perk up. *That would be good.*

"I'll sew it right now. I have time, but you have to stop attacking me."

Maybe.

She walks over and picks up the stuffed bunny and the tail and fetches the sewing kit.

I watch her closely as she sews them together, mending the bunny like new. I reach out for it, but she snatches it away. "You leave this alone."

I stare at it.

"Not yours. Come, I'll get you a snack."

Okay. I eat and curl up and take another nap. Keeping one ear alert for food. Rae talks as she works and hums too.

The park radio squawks, waking me up. Boston, calling for a ranger. We both look at it. A few minutes later, Bob calls for backup.

"Wonder what she has going," Rae says. "We'll ask, she's due home soon."

Then Bob calls Kevlar on the radio and requests a phone call.

"That's interesting. Too bad we can't hear what they say on the phone."

I return to my nap and dream of riding the reddish egret until Rae's complaints wake me up.

She is in a panic. She has called Boston a bunch of times with no answer. "Where is she. She was supposed to be home to tell me if the turkeys are done. I'm not sure how to tell. I know I'm supposed to push a thigh, but I don't know what I'm supposed to see or feel."

Rae's desperate and keeps looking at the door, but it doesn't open. "Where is Boston?" she says, over and over. "She should be here."

But Boston doesn't come home.

The phone rings and Rae jumps for it. "Boston, thank goodness you finally called. You were supposed to be home thirty minutes ago to do the turkeys. How do I tell if they're done? Where are you? Why aren't you here? Why aren't you answering your phone?" She strings all the questions together and I hear Boston trying to break in. They are talking over each other.

"Stop Rae. Listen. Stop. Rae," she says in her stern deep schoolteacher voice.

Rae stops.

Boston says, "We have a situation in the campground. I can't get home. You're going to have to do it yourself. Turkeys should be done. Check them."

"What? I don't know how to. Don't make me. You need to come home and help."

"Listen, Rae. You can. I'll walk you through it."

"What about Kev? Can't he do it? Please."

"Kev is here. We're both tied up. Calm down. Calm down."

"Okay. Okay. What happened?"

"My fault. I caught some people driving on the grass in the tent camping area to load canoes. When I went to stop them, I found they had collected about a hundred protected air plants. I called in Bob and then we called in all the rangers. We're going to be here all afternoon."

"Please come home."

"Can't. But the whole meal will be delayed because everyone is working here. To test the turkey, use the thermometer, it has the temperature for turkey on it. Poke the thigh with a fork, juices should be clear. I'll get there as soon as I can." She hangs up.

Rae sits. "Juices should run clear," she tells me.

I watch her stab the turkey, first with the thermometer, then with a fork, but she's doesn't get me a snack.

"Tiger."

What?

"We have to check the turkeys in the chickee, they should be about done. This one needs another few minutes. Come on. Snacks when we get back."

Okay. More snacks.

"I have a toy for you to play with while I work."

She pulls the toy from her pocket and waves it under my nose. A catnip mouse. I inhale deeply, really good fresh catnip. I will follow her anywhere.

She tosses it to me inside the chickee, dropping it in front of me. But I ignore it until she squeezes it and waves it under my nose again. "Here Tiger. This is a great toy. Please try it."

Begging works. The lady learns quickly. Doesn't mean she can buy me off. Or I guess it does.

I attack my mouse while she checks the turkey. Making

happy sounds, she turns off the oven and pulls the turkeys out one by one and sets them on the counter.

"Boston asked me to put the plastic tablecloths on the picnic tables, so you play."

Right, I'll play. Sniffff. Smells good. I look at the bird closest to the edge of the counter and walk over, stand on my back toes and stretch up the cabinet. Can just look across the countertop. It's right there. I can smell it. Can't reach it from down here. Maybe I can jump.

"Tiger. Get away from there. Go play with your toy."

Sure. I'll do that. I sit and wait for her to turn away.

"I'm watching you. You can have turkey when we get home."

Well. I don't know. I can have turkey now. Here. She can't watch me every minute.

But she covers the turkeys with tin foil and puts them back in the oven and waves the mouse under my nose. I snatch it away from her and pounce and forget about the turkeys. Holding it with my front paws, I tear it with my back claws. Bite an ear hard. I work on the mouse a long time and I think I must be a little drunk from the catnip because I let her carry me home.

"You're almost as heavy as one of those turkeys, but easier to carry."

She's got me upside down, like a baby. If I were sober, I'd be embarrassed, but now, I'm happy to let her carry me with the mouse in my paw. At home, she sets me down in my chair and I sleep.

Rae's wail wakes me up. "No. I can't do it."

Three Turkeys

"You need to make the gravy," Boston says on the speaker phone. "It's simple. Make two batches. Just make a roux, add the juices from the giblets."

"What about chopped liver and neck meat?"

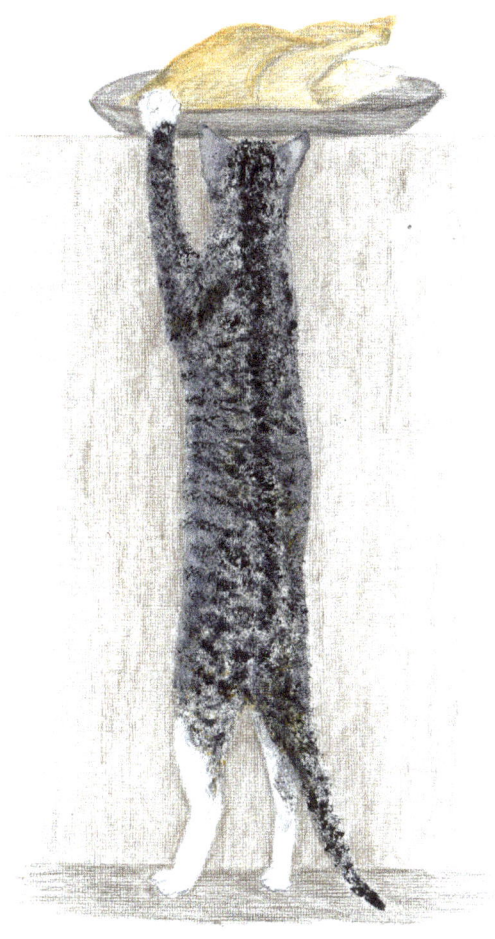

"Put those in and Kev will add pan drippings when we get home."

"Yeah, yeah, yeah. I know how to make a roux." Resigned. "Can I call if I run into trouble? Or are you too busy?" she says while getting out the flour.

"Call. I'll answer if I can or call you back. Thank you, thank you. You are a life saver. Want to make a pie?"

"What? Are you crazy? A pie? How can I make a pie? Where am I supposed to cook it? The ovens are full. Where do I get the ingredients?"

"I have all the ingredients for your millionaire pie, so two pies actually. The guys were going to make some desserts, but they're all here working. Bob was supposed to make a pumpkin pie. Please?"

"Oh. Well, I guess I could. I have nothing else to do."

"If you can, it would be great. Bye."

"She hung up, Tiger. We're on our own."

Humph. She's on her own. I'm just here for the food.

She shrugs her shoulders. "Oh, well. Nothing much easier them millionaire pie. But first I better get the roux done."

She measures and stirs and spills some juice from the giblets when she adds them to the roux, and I help by cleaning the floor.

"You know, Tiger, you're a big help. Someone to talk to. You listen well."

I don't think she realizes she's talking to me like I'm a person.

She passes me a piece of liver which I take out of

her hand delicately, and then she tosses down some turkey meat.

She's a nice person. Caring.

"Millionaire pie is simple and pretty and one batch makes two pies." She talks as she hunts through cupboards and the freezer. "Here we go, everything is here, even premade pie crusts. Smart girl, my sister." She pours and mixes things together.

I watch, she may have more turkey for me.

What? She ate something. Just popped it in her mouth. I move closer and sniff.

Cherries. Yuk. Sweet stuff. I go back to my mouse.

Rae's chatting away. I'm beginning to find it comforting.

"Okay. While the pies are chilling, I think I'll make another pie, maybe banana cream with chocolate. It doesn't need to cook either. And I'm going to make my famous dip. Boston has the ingredients and she said some of the guys are bringing chips. If you're going to put on a party, you should have all the courses. We need dip. Actually," she looks down at me, "I'm afraid to stop."

No turkey. I return to my nap.

Boston comes in, yelling, "Company's coming. Tiger. Rae. Company's coming. We got company. They're right behind me. Two for overnight. They'll crash in the living room."

She draws in a breath. "It smells wonderful in here." Her eyes get big as she looks over the counter. "Wow. You made an extra cake. You're wonderful. You have saved the day. You know that, right?"

Rae shrugs. "I got bored. Made my carrot casserole and gourmet onions and my sweet potato surprise. Had plenty of time. What happened?"

"Told you, I saw some idiots drive their vehicles across the tent camping area. That's dangerous because people sleep on the ground. Anyhow, I went over to talk to them and chase them off and they were unloading air plants from their canoes to their vehicles. Bromeliads and orchids including three very rare white ghost orchids," she says outraged. "The three ghost orchids made me want to kick them. The men, not the plants. Ghost orchids are very rare and shouldn't be disturbed."

She always talks about ghost orchids with a tone of reverence, because they're endangered. White flowers with two long tendrils which float in the breeze, like a ghost. To me, they look like frog legs. For some reason, the plant doesn't have any leaves, but like other orchids, its roots attach to the host tree.

"I called Bob and when he saw the canoes full of bromeliads and orchids, he called for reinforcements."

She smiles. "The idiots figured, since the vehicles were already there at the water's edge, they ought to be able to load the canoes. But Bob just shook his head and made them drive their vehicles back to the pavement. He made the dumb clucks carry the canoes to the parking lot and load them on a ranger trailer. Then, he confiscated them. It was neat. Then the idiots wanted to keep the plants. Can you believe?"

Her smile got wider. "Those men were maaad. When

Bob told them, they needed to come to the ranger station, AND, they were going to be cited - ticketed - and fined, *per plant*, it got really interesting. 'Ranger Station or we carry you handcuffed to town and jail,' Bob said."

"Wow," Rae says. "Wish I'd been there."

"Yeah. We called Research to take possession of the plants. Maybe a hundred of them. Ned, the researcher, will have the exact number. And while Bob dealt with the jerks at the station, Ned supervised the loading of the plants and their safe placement into a truck Kev brought. Took a long time to move them, and then inventory, and store them safely. That's why we're so late. Two of the research guys came back with us to eat turkey, spend the night, get an early start in the morning as soon as it's light to return the ghost orchids to the backcountry as soon as possible. Ned knows a place where they grow."

"I'd like to see those," Rae says.

"Ned's staying here tonight, so you can look at them in the morning. How's everything here. Looks like you've been busy."

"Like I said. Got bored. Cooked. Tiger helped. You know three people have called your landline to say Catfish told them the chickee was cancelled, that there wasn't any turkey. I told them there are three perfectly cooked twenty pounders. Plus, lots of stuffing, gravy, and dessert."

"He spread that rumor before he disappeared. Who cares. We announced over the park radio the party is a go. I really owe you. The whole community does. These seasonals have nowhere to go but the chickee. Without you we'd be eating chips and dips. Oooh, you even made some salsa dip. Thank you."

A pack of stinky men, hooting and laughing, tumbles through the door all noise and excitement, all talking at once. One of the men heads to me.

"Nice kitty," he says and reaches out.

"Don't," Kevlar hollers too late as I swipe and snarl.

The man jumps back fast, like the reddish egret.

I smile at him and he moves back another foot, behind Kevlar.

"Tiger. Bad cat," Boston admonishes me. "This is a friend. Ned." She turns to Ned. "I'm sorry Ned, did he get you? I'm afraid I trained him to stand up for himself when he was young."

Ned shakes his hand, holds it in front of him. "Just a scratch. Cats generally like me."

"Not this cat," Rae says from the stove. "He's mean. But he can be bribed with treats."

I think she shouldn't tell secrets. Well, okay, maybe she should. It's okay for him to offer me treats. Chicken. Or maybe beef. Both. Or that piece of giblet Rae's holding out. That would work.

I check to make sure he understands, but he's staring at Rae, holding out his hand. "He drew blood."

I never touched him.

Rae takes his hand in both of hers. "He did."

I barely touched him. I pulled my scratch.

They both stare at each other. He wraps his fingers around her hand.

"Ned, my sister, Rachel. Rachel, Ned. From Research. Our botanist and air plant specialist. The other guy is Kane."

Rae's not listening. "Sit here and I'll get the first aid kit. He's scratched me a few times too."

They just look at each other.

"Something smells great," the other guy says and heads for the kitchen.

"Let me see." Kevlar follows him and they both sigh when Kane opens the oven.

I walk over to look.

Kane says, "Turkey. Perfectly brown. That's a beautiful sight. Gottta tell you Boston, I wasn't totally convinced. Catfish sure made it sound like the chickee was cancelled. Glad I asked. I wasn't really looking forward to chips and beer on Thanksgiving."

Boston agrees. "He made a mistake. My sister does good work. And from the look of the desserts on the counter, and the pots on the stove, she does a lot of work."

"Did a lot of work." Kevlar corrects. "I think she's done." He motions to Rae and Ned, still standing in the kitchen holding hands and looking at each other.

"Good thing we like Ned, because he might be part of the family soon."

I like him. He let me scratch him.

BIG BIRDS

I'm helping Boston clean up after last night's outdoor BBQ. She's policing the area - picking up trash. I'm licking the grill utensils.

The party ended suddenly when the Rangers were called out for an emergency. We brought all the leftover food and drinks inside but left the cleanup for daylight. I got some good eats at the party. Kevlar snuck me some rib meat. Don't really like the BBQ sauce, but beggars can't be choosers. Not that I begged. Maine Coon cats don't beg. We're strong, smart cats. We hunt. I snared a hunk of chicken when no one was looking, before it was glazed with that sauce. I was quick. Chicken is my favorite.

Boston comes over to me and looks at the utensils. "I'll take these in and wash them. Though they look clean."

I cleaned them. I licked them all myself. Dried juices, no meat.

She puts them aside and I wander off, hunting.

There's no food at all out here. None. So now I'm officially bored.

Wait. A bone over there.

She isn't watching, and I walk over to it.

"Tiger. Don't eat that."

Bummer. Those words in that tone mean she is going to take it away.

I put both front paws on it. *Mine.*

"Tiger." She comes closer. "Let me see."

My head stays low protecting my catch, but I raise my eyes to look up at her.

"That's a pretty big bone," she says, "but it's already been chewed clean. I saw Killer with it last night."

She walks away.

What? Yuk. Sluggo chewed it? People call him Killer, but he prefers Sluggo. He's a dog. And she's right. No meat. Not even a smell. Not that I'd eat anything left over by Sluggo.

Frustrated, I decide to check out the strange huffing noises coming from the other side of the sea grapes and palmettos. Curious sounds. Kind of oof, grunt, hak. Coughing, flapping, ruffling sounds. Bound to be some entertainment. Should I walk around or go through the clumps of palmetto? Choices, choices. If I go around, I avoid the sharp spines on the radiating palmetto fronds. But cats don't go around. Especially Maine Coon cats. Besides, through is the most direct route and will give me cover.

I look back. Boston is picking up the bone, dropping it in her trash bag. I duck under a palmetto and walk straight into a cobweb. Well, darn. Sticky things. Hate them.

Oh, I hope there's not a spider on me. They make me

itchy. My skin twitches at the thought of one crawling on me with all his skinny pointy little feet. Stupid spiders. The Golden Orb spider. Ugly things. They always seem to only come in large size, so I'd feel one if it was on me. Boston says they're harmless and get their name from the golden silk they use to spin their stupid sticky webs. She says the stuff is really strong. If sticky is strong, yeah. And it's not gold and doesn't look gold on my fur. Yuk.

Darn. The web is stuck on my whiskers and eyelashes. I drag my right paw over it and wipe it off and the stupid thing sticks to my paw. Bummer.

I shake my paw, but the web sticks. At least I got the thing off my face. Webs aren't as bad as beggar lice. Beggar lice always come in tribes, never just one, and they stick everywhere. I hate them. Hate cobwebs too.

Disgusted, I wiggle through some more palmettos to the other side and find a bunch of buzzards or vultures. I'm not sure which is the right name. They're scavengers and eat dead stuff. Dead animals.

No one and nothing eats buzzard. So, no snack for me.

Right now, they are squawking and grunting, hopping up and down and shoving each other. Fighting for a spot at the buzzard buffet. What the heck are they fighting over? I don't smell any animals, alive, half alive, or dead. BBQ? Leftover BBQ chicken?

I step closer. Sniff. And remember I got all the chicken last night.

A few feet away, two of the big birds are facing off. Tugging opposite ends of a long morsel. Huh. They slap each other with their wings. It's not food though. Looks like a sock. A black sock. A dead stinky sock. Stupid buzzards. They caught a dead sock.

That's the way it works with vultures. One guy says, "Oh, hey, supper." And then they all try to be first at the dinner table and no one notices it's a sock. Stupid birds. Makes me smile. Could be fun after all. Fighting over a sock. Though, the whiff I just got, does stink like something dead. One wins the tug-a-war and jumps away with the prize, shaking it.

The rest of them are still pecking angrily at a mound of stuff on the ground. Curious, I edge closer. Sniff. Hmmm. I almost recognize the smell, and it's not dead animal.

"Tiger? Where are you? You're not supposed to wander off. What's all this racket?"

I stay quiet on my stomach watching. Boston walks around the sea grapes and stops.

"Oh. Buzzards." She takes a step closer and three fly off. She studies them. "See, Tiger, it's easy to identify them. The turkey buzzard is sort of brown and has the red head and the black vulture has the black head."

You would think he would be called a red buzzard. But that would be too simple. Hard to decide which is uglier with their wrinkly bald heads.

"They are ugly and clumsy on the ground, but in the air, it's a whole different story. They're magnificent in the air." She watches them circle low. "They catch the updrafts and soar with the wind, looking for food. You can tell them apart in the air too. The red has white all along the back edge of its six-foot wingspan, the black has shorter wings, five feet, with white wing tips, shorter tails too.

"The blacks are better soarers and have better eyesight, but the reds have a better sense of smell and usually find the food first. The blacks follow along. Both sexes look the same, unusual for birds. They're bald so they can keep their heads clean when they stick them inside something dead."

Are they born bald or do they shave their heads like Bob?

"What are they eating?" she asks and takes another step closer, frowning. "What's that gray stuff?" She takes another step.

Two more of the birds squawk and take off and join a bunch circling overhead, the rest nervously back up a few feet, protesting.

Her eyes squint and her mouth turns down in a frown as she looks kind of sideways at the mess. "Black eyed peas?" She sounds like she doesn't believe it and walks closer with both eyes open. "Black eyed peas and ham hocks. Is that what they're after? The ham hocks? Bob was going to take the leftovers home with him last night."

I walk closer too. *Yep. Ham hocks. Always been fond of them. In fact, they're my favorite. I edge closer to a ham hock lying in the grass nearby.*

"Tiger. Get away from that. You have your own food."

No I don't. Breakfast was a long time ago. I hover over the ham hock. But, truthfully, it doesn't look very appetizing.

"How did they get that? And what does that bird have in its beak?" She moves closer to the bird with the sock. "Eww." She makes a big distasteful grimace, wrinkling her nose. "Not sure I really want to see. But the other buzzard wants it."

She moves closer to the sock which gives me a chance to sniff the ham hock.

The bird backs off, dropping the sock.

Hmm. That might be more interesting. I run ahead of her and get to it first. *Eww is right.* It's a really stinky sock. Not food stinky. But foot stinky.

"A sock," she says. "There's something in it. Hope it's not a foot."

I head back to the ham hock.

"I see you," she says not even looking at me. "Don't touch that."

"Hey, Ola? What's going on out there?" Bob calls from the parking area.

"We're behind the sea grapes," she replies and whispers to me, "we'll get Bob to pick up the stinky sock." Then she yells through the trees. "Come help."

He walks around and stops when he sees the birds gathered around the gray mess. "Oh, wow, is that my black-eyed peas and ham hocks. I so wanted them for lunch today. We got that call-out last night at the end of the party, and I took off forgetting I had that pot of peas on the tailgate. Guess it bounced off and rolled. And then we were out most of the night on that hospital run. What a mess. Sorry about this. I'll get it cleaned up." He looks around at the buzzards and shakes his head.

"Guess I don't have to worry about cleaning it up. Let the natural scavengers do it."

He's not getting my ham hock. I crouch over it.

"Don't worry Tiger. I consider you a natural scavenger." He picks up the pot lid. "Didn't even break. Where's the pot? You see it?"

"Right there, under the branches. I'll get it." Boston

motions to the sock and quickly picks up the pot. "I think you need to check out that sock. The buzzards were fighting over it and there's something in it."

He walks over and looks down and frowns. "I could hold the pot, Boston, and you can pick up the sock."

She hugs the pot close to her. "I got it. And I'm not touching that sock. The vultures had their beaks all over it and there's something chunky in it. If it's a foot, it's a law-enforcement problem."

Huh. Guess they're like the birds and need to go through a ritual. One of not getting the sock. I sniff the ham hock. Doesn't really smell good. Old. Has ants on it. Ants are okay. But…

"I'm afraid to touch it," Bob says. "Got a glove or pickup stick?"

"Give me a minute. Don't leave or those birds will get the sock." With a nod she takes the pot and disappears behind the trees, comes back with her pick-up stick. She looks down at my catch and hands me a treat from her pocket. "Tiger I'll give you a snack. Leave that."

I give the ham hock a pat and sniff my paw. Lick it. Ugh. Decide to settle down to enjoy my snack and am cleaning my paws when they both walk by me. Boston has the sock grasped in the pick-up stick holding it out to the side away from her. They are still squabbling over who has to touch it.

"Get your gloves. I know you have a whole box of rubber gloves in your vehicle. Go get those."

"Forgot all about them," he says opening the truck

door and leaning in. Comes out pulling the gloves on. He pulls down the tailgate and sits.

"Hand it over." He takes it gently from her with tongs, lays it on a small tarp and bends over it with scissors.

"Surgical scissors?" Boston asks snorting, "it's a dirty wet sock which has been tossed around by buzzards."

"Only ones I have and what were you planning to do? Turn it upside down and squeeze it like a tube of toothpaste?"

"Well, yeah. That's what I was getting ready to do."

"Watch an expert, girl, while I slice this guy down the side and open it like unfolding an omelet."

I jump on the tailgate to be close. Don't want to miss anything. Might be some toys.

He puts the sock on its side and carefully slices along the edge starting at the top, around the heel and toe. He lays down the scissors and grabs the heel part, opening it away from him. He just looks.

What. What? I lift my head but can't see over.

"What," Boston says, "show us."

Yeah.

He unfolds the top, opening the sock all the way, and we both look.

"Is that a roll of money?" Boston asks reaching out a hand.

I reach out a paw for the shiny ring.

"No." He gently slaps her hand and I snatch my paw back.

"Oh, right." She puts her hand down, fingers still reaching out. "Is that a roll of hundred-dollar bills?"

"Looks like. Better get pictures before we disturb anything."

"Like the vultures didn't jumble everything up," she quips.

"I know they shook everything up, but we still do it by the book."

"You're right. You're right. I just wanted to touch it. And, yes, I know I can't do that."

"Glove up while I get pictures and then maybe we can look."

Can I have that shiny ring?

Bob pokes the roll of money with tweezers and they both bend down to look closer.

"Date on that outside one is old," she says. "That's a pretty thick roll. Can't tell if it's all hundreds."

"Looks like hundreds. A bunch." He pokes the ring. "A ring, small."

That would be fun. I could roll that around. I move closer, but he notices and blocks me.

"And a watch. Both look like a woman's small size. Both with inscriptions. And the watch," he pokes it again, "could have an ID number."

"What's that band around the money?" Boston asks pointing with a knuckle.

"I think, yes, it is. It is an old POW/MIA bracelet with the soldier's name. You know, the Prisoner of War/Missing in Action bracelets they sold back in the 1960s to increase public awareness about Americans still being held prisoner, or missing, and unaccounted for from the Vietnam War. My Mom has one. It's how she met my Dad."

Boston looks up at him. "No way. Your mom had your dad's bracelet?"

Bob looks embarrassed. "Well, sort of. Might tell you the story someday. We may be able to trace this bracelet."

I reach out to the ring and get pushed back again.

"Now. Tell now."

He shakes his head.

Is this another version of the buzzard dance?

"Tell," Boston repeats her order, but Bob is ignoring her demand and says, "The bracelet is tight around the money. All the juggling by the buzzards didn't shake any bills loose. Guess I better call the District Ranger and tell him what we have."

I lose interest. No food, and they won't let me play with the toys. Besides, something is going on behind the stand of trees on the shoreline. Birds are acting funny.

I jump off the tailgate and trot across the grass as three birds head in for a landing in the trees on the bay side but swoop up and over the trees to settle on the land side. Ibis. White birds with a red curved-down beak. Something scaring them from the sea side of the trees. Two more repeat the maneuver as I walk toward them.

Bob calls Catfish on the radio and gets no response. Jackson answers though and asks if Bob wants help.

"We're out front. Come on down," Bob tells him.

"Huh. Got it," Boston says looking at her cell.

"What?" Bob asks.

"The bracelet. Charles Monroe Sutherland, MIA, January 7, 1975. Currently lives in Florida City."

"How did you find that out?"

"Googled him and searched through social media. His grandson brags about him on his blog."

"So, he's still alive. This wouldn't be his bracelet. He wouldn't carry his own bracelet."

"We can ask. Monroe and Sutherland are local family names. You could call. Or first search your wonderful law enforcement database."

"I'll get someone checking backcountry permits, float plans. See if any vehicles on the ramp or in the campground are abandoned. We haven't been notified of anyone overdue."

I'm most of the way to the trees. Not going to crouch down and slither on my belly. Don't really want to, the grass is wet. Besides whatever is out there won't be scared off if I walk over. Can't be a gator. If he is sunning in the water, the birds wouldn't have tried to land on the water side. If he is on land, they would have flown farther away. Can't be a panther, same reasoning.

Could be a bobcat. They sort of look like me. Except they stand taller, have short fur and aren't fluffy. All muscle and sinew hanging out. They are black and tan with very little white. And have only a short, short tail. A bobbed tail, Boston calls it. They're born with it. Or without it. Hmm. Maybe they don't look like me.

Yeah, it could be a bobcat or maybe a coon. A racoon. I don't like raccoons. They're sissy and prissy. And mean. They are fluffy like Maine Coon cats, but they have a black mask over their eyes. Lets you know right away not to trust them. Because they're sneaky. And they smell.

I'm still thinking about not crouching down when I hear the clatter of Sluggo's toenails on the stairs back by the truck. Of course, if Jackson comes out, so does Sluggo. I look back and he's running to the truck, bouncing up and down. He spins in a circle and turns and sees me. Gives a happy yip and charges.

Jackson yells, "Get back here Killer."

Boston calls me.

I wait until Sluggo is about four feet away and stand up, arch my back high, point my tail to the sky, and snarl.

He stumbles over his feet. Stops. Turns around and runs back.

I don't snigger, Maine Coon cats don't snigger. I lean down and clean my front paw while I snigger.

Sluggo notices the buzzards and charges, scattering them left, right, and up. He races around with his nose on the ground sniffing where they've been. Finds a ham hock and gulps it down, ants, bones and all before Jackson reaches him and lifts him off the ground. "Bad dog," he says and they head toward me by the water. Jackson sounds a little like Boston when she admonishes me but is secretly impressed by what I did.

Jackson sets Sluggo down and the little dog charges with a howl, startling the birds right out of the trees. There is a scratching, scrabbling noise on the other side of the trees and I scoot under the branches.

A coon galumphs away and quickly climbs the nearest mangrove. Partway up, he stops and looks down at us with his masked face.

Sluggo jumps up but can't reach him. Yipping, barking, he bounces up and down. Jackson walks around the trees with a stern, "Killer." Catches him in mid-leap.

I'm checking through the stuff spilled out of a cooler and scattered around on the ground, but no food or toys.

Boston comes through the trees. "Guess we know where that sock came from. I see the mate over there." She points. But I'm already pushing it with my paw. Another lumpy sock.

"Leave that alone, Tiger," she says, "it's probably evidence. Come here, I have another treat."

I back off a step. She should bring the treat to me.

"I'll call Bob have him bring the truck, camera, and evidence bags," Jackson says. "We'll stay here and scare off predators."

Boston snorts. "Yeah, right." She walks over and gives me the treat, mostly to get a better look at the sock. Then she examines the cooler, not touching anything. "Looks like the guy stored his stuff in the cooler." She looks over the bay. "Must have washed overboard, though it would be hard for something to wash overboard in this skinny water. Think he was heading for Snake Bight maybe?"

Snake Bight is an inlet behind the housing area and the water is only a foot or two deep. Skinny. All over. I went there with her in the boat once. Talk about boring.

Bob drives the truck over. "The Sutherland guy is home," he says. "Entrance station called. Says he does fish out of here. You know the truck, an old green Chevy. Blue tailgate. Guy has a flats boat."

"Yeah. Good fisherman. Always brings back just enough for supper," Boston says. "Fun to talk to."

They take pictures of the cooler, video too, and then

lift things one by one placing them in sacks and labelling them.

"Looks like it washed ashore and came open. Or the coon opened it. Seen them do that," Bob says. "Now we just have to find out who owns it and why they have a roll of hundred-dollar bills. Strange to bring that kind of money birding or camping."

"The other sock has stuff in it," Boston says, and Bob gives it the same treatment as the first, with Jackson videotaping. "Chapstick, sunscreen. Nothing else."

Strange noises. I point my ears toward the clump of mangroves farther down the bank. Squint, to hear better. Still can't identify. But Sluggo sees me, looks, and goes on alert. Puts his nose in the air and sniffs.

And howls, "Awwoooowww."

"Killer," Jackson yells. "Stop that."

Howling like a crazy dog, Sluggo charges, dodges around the trees and disappears behind them.

I head that way cautiously.

"Woof. Woof."

"Killer. Come back here," Jackson hollers.

A weak voice says, "Hey puppy."

Boston scoops me up and we peer around the trees. Sluggo is standing in front of a skinny old lady sitting on the ground with one of those strange canoes in her lap. She smells like Florida Bay muck. That smell humans stir up walking through the skinny water on the mudflat.

Tail wagging, Sluggo tries to lick her face.

"Good doggie. Good doggie." She pats his head.

Jackson heads for her. "Hey ma'am. You okay?" He leans over.

"Yeah," she says.
"My name's Jackson."
"Myra. Myra Hayes. Really pleased to meet you."
"Your leg looks bloody. Okay if I take a look at it?"

"Yeah. I cut it on a shell in the muck."

Jackson bends over the lady's leg and touches the cut. She groans.

"Sorry." He continues feeling her leg gently. "What happened?"

"Stupid. I was stupid."

"How?"

"Had a big fish on the line and was totally involved in reeling it in, wasn't watching where he was taking me. Kayak ran aground, tipped over. Fish got loose. Got messed up trying to right myself. Lost my gear on the bow. Got out to retrieve it. Sank down in the muck. Everything had floated off by the time I got my boat upright. Couldn't get back in it." The lady shakes her head in disgust. "Just feeling really foolish. Got stuck in the muck and tripped and fell. Cut my leg. Had to use the kayak for support the last few feet to shore."

"That must be your stuff down the shoreline."

"You found my stuff?" she says hopefully.

"Yeah. If you had black socks. One with a bracelet in it."

"Thank God. Don't want to lose that MIA bracelet. Had it since the war. Keep Charles with me. I haven't forgotten"

"Well, Charles Monroe Sutherland is no longer MIA. He lives in town. You should give him a call; tell him you have his bracelet. You'd probably like each other. He fishes the flats."

"Really? I might do that. Who said every cloud has a

silver lining?" She pauses. "The bracelet was around a roll of bills. There was a watch and ring."

"Money's still there. Jewelry too. Lot of money for a kayaking trip."

"I was heading for Key Largo, straight across the flats. Need money for a motel room."

Sluggo is licking the lady's face. I guess he likes the Florida Bay muck since the woman is covered in it. But dogs lick faces.

"Doctor is going to have to look at this leg."

"Yeah, figured. Don't know how I'm going to get back to town."

"We'll take you. Got the ambulance coming. But first we'll get your kayak in the truck."

The Rangers collect everything. And Sluggo is still licking the lady. He's making her happy. The ambulance arrives and Bob and Jackson load the woman up.

"Can the doggie come with us?' she asks. "He's a real friendly guy. Can't tell you how happy I was to see him."

The men look at each other, and Bob shrugs. "Okay. But he can't go in the hospital."

"Thanks."

Boston watches them go and then puts me down. "Wow. What a day. Let's finish our clean-up and get lunch."

Hope its tuna. Or maybe bacon. I could eat bacon. Or chicken.

I follow her home, because I am hungry. Maybe it will be tuna.

TAKE YOUR CAT
TO WORK DAY

Bob glides the ranger squad car to a stop at the campground kiosk and rolls down his window. "Hey there."

"Did Catfish send you after all?" Boston asks hopefully.

"No. Was he supposed to? Do you have a problem?"

"Not a problem. A feeling. He said he wasn't interested and hung up on me. He didn't send you?"

"No. What's the problem, excuse me, the feeling? Is that what you told Catfish? You had a feeling? I'm not surprised he hung up on you. So what is this feeling? You mean like something you touched like a snakeskin? Or something inside like a tummy ache?"

Boston laughs. "Yeah, like that, a gut feeling. About a wrong guy."

"What wrong guy? You mean he went the wrong way? Or…" he sees me and stops with a double-take. "What is Tiger doing on the counter in there?"

Boston kind of straightens her shoulders and gets all

defensive. "Well, it's Take Your Cat to Work Day, so I brought my cat to work."

And I'm having a good time. I have all the comforts of home. A milk dish, three toys, and my pillow, a litter pan, and attention from the campers who notice me. I'm free to wander around the kiosk, but Boston says I can't sneak out her window when it's open because I might run off and get lost.

Like that would happen. Sneak out sure, but I wouldn't get lost. Maine Coon cats don't get lost. We are hunters and have an excellent sense of direction.

Bob snickers. "It is not. You made that up. If there was a Take Your Cat to Work Day, I'd have brought Wolf."

Is so take your cat to work. And who cares if Wolf gets to go to work. I don't like Wolf, Bob's cat. He's mean. We are enemies. We don't fight anymore, because both Bob and Boston have laid down the law, no cat fights. So, we don't fight, we stare and glower. But I could beat him.

"Why is Tiger in the kiosk?" he asks again.

She says defensively, "Actually, it's our turn for the rental inspection and I was afraid someone would leave a door open and let Tiger out, so I brought him with me. He's lapping up all the attention he's getting from campers."

Bob laughs. "The inspectors were in my place yesterday. They propped the door open. Wolf went out twice. Good thing I was home."

"Then you understand."

"Drat. This is the first TYCTWD and me and Wolf missed it."

"Well it's actually the second."

"You've brought him here before?"

"No. Long time ago and far, far, away. On another job. I brought him to school with me."

"Technically that would be Take You Cat to School Day. How did your teacher like that?"

"I was the teacher. Summer school, third grade. Wasn't my plan, but we were on our way home from a weekend holiday and he was in the car and I didn't have time to take him home, so I took him to work." She pauses. "It didn't go too well. "The kids squealed in delight, jabbering all at once, even before we were in the room. Grabbing for him. I tried to lift him out of their reach, but he's heavy."

"No kidding."

"You want to hear this or not?"

Yeah. You want to hear this story? Tell it. Tell it. I love this story. I'm the star.

He nods.

Her lips curve up. "Good. I earn free beers with this tale." She nods to herself. "Anyhow, I set him on a table, but the kids kept reaching trying to touch and pat and grab. He swatted at one hand and then another. You know how short tempered he is."

"Yeah. He doesn't like to be touched."

"He snarled. He arched his back. Brought his tail around front. Ruffled his fur. Laid his ears half-flat. Opened his mouth wide. Growled.

She laughs and pats me.

It wasn't a real snarl. I wasn't angry or scared. Just wanted them to back off. Heck, I didn't even have my ears flattened, just lowered. I only hissed at them. Well, maybe snarled.

"The closest kid stumbled back, knocking into two others who stumbled into six or eight more. And like dominoes they all toppled over, taking down a few extra kids with them. I had visions of ambulances squealing to a stop out in front of the school."

It was cool. All those kids tumbling. And I made it happen. I preen a little.

"I reached for the nearest kid in the pile to help him up and the one under him screamed. I saw myself in the unemployment line." She pauses again.

She has the story down for full effect.

"A big kid yelled; **He blew on me. Hard. Like a tornado. Knocked me over. He's a Supercat.**"

Yep. Maine Coon Supercat. That's me.

"The kid beside him squealed awestruck, *I saw flames. Flames shot out of his mouth, like Godzilla*. A third, crying, held his arm out to me and I worried it might be broken. This little kid hurt because I brought the cat to school. But then he wailed, **He burned me. You need to rub it Miss Teacher. Make it better**. Three more chimed in, **Me too. Me too. He burned me with fire from his mouth**."

Boston giggles. "Their stories got wilder. The littlest kid said, **He's a dragon. A ninja dragon, breathing fire. I saw him breathe fire. Like a flame thrower**. And a cat star was born. I tried, but I couldn't convince them cats don't breathe fire. Even dragon cats."

I can breathe fire if I want.

"It was pretty funny."

It was fun. Wolf can't do that.

Boston laughs. "After that, no one came near him. But the word got around during recess about the fire-breathing-dragon-cat which could knock over a kid with his breath and there was a steady stream of kids and teachers to our classroom door. And from the safety of the doorway they whispered and pointed at the fire-breathing-dragon-cat."

She brushes a hand down my head. "Tiger was in heaven. One of the teachers told the kids he was a Maine Coon cat and he seemed to like that better than Godzilla or Ninja dragon."

I smile proudly at Bob from my Maine Coon cat pose with my ears up. I don't have the ear tufts most Coon cats have, I'm not sure why, but I do have the aristocratic attitude.

He snorts. "Cute story. I'll buy you a beer after work."

And me a shrimp?

"But Catfish won't like it. If he knew your cat was here, he'd send a Ranger quick enough."

"Oh. Don't tell him. He doesn't need to know."

"He won't hear it from me. But you should be prepared, a camper might tell him."

She scoffs. "No worries. He doesn't talk to campers."

"Tell me about your feeling."

"Just a guy who gave me the creeps."

"What guy?"

"I don't want to get you in trouble."

Bob sighs. "Just tell me about the guy. Who?"

"The guy down at the end of the walk-in." She points. "That camper parked there. He's wrong."

"That's it?" Bob asks.

"Go look. I bet he's already broken some rule. I'm not fey, but he's evil."

"Who's Faye?"

"What? Oh. Not Faye as in a girl's name, fey as in clairvoyant, all seeing, psychic."

He shakes his head laughing and taps a finger to his Stetson brim. "Well, I'm going to take a swing through the campground. Maybe I'll get a feeling." He drives into C Loop, comes out a few minutes later and turns into A Loop, drives around it and heads into the Walk-in tent camping. Slows as he passes the camper and heads back out.

"Guess he didn't get a feeling," Boston says to herself and picks up some paperwork. I slap my stuffed red frog around the countertop. It accidently tumbles on her papers.

Bob knocks on the backdoor startling both of us. "Let me in," he hollers. "Have to use the land-line."

He doesn't mean a line going into the dirt. He means the phone on the counter attached to a wire which goes into a wall.

He picks up the phone receiver. "I parked back behind the restroom and walked over. Didn't want anyone to see me."

"You agree with me," Boston says. "The guy's wrong, my gut's right."

My gut says food and I look sadly at my empty food dish.

"Yeah. Don't know about wrong, but something is way off with your camper. Definitely breaking the rules. Guy is parked on the grass. Left ruts where he drove across it. And there's a black pickup with an empty go-fast boat trailer parked beside him. Cigarette boat trailer."

"I saw that come in, a Dodge? Big fat guy. Black hair

and long beard. He's not registered, and he didn't stop, just slowed down. Figured he was visiting someone or just looking around. Don't see too many go-fast boats in Flamingo."

Bob's talking into the phone, "Doug. I'm in the campground kiosk. Can you locate the District Ranger for me? He's somewhere at HQ and not answering his cell. We have a problem. Keep radio silence. Call me back here at the campground."

He turns to Boston. "The tag on the camper comes back to a blue Chevy Silverado. The truck tag should be on a white Toyota Camry. No tag on the boat trailer. You may really be fey." He leans against the desk. "I could stop and cite him, probably arrest on what we have, but the go-fast boat trailer could mean something totally different. Do you know if they launched it here?"

She shakes her head. "All I know is the truck came in with the empty trailer, went down through the walk in area."

"I need someone in civilian clothes to ask around the marina."

Boston says, "I can call the marina. If someone launched a Cigarette here, they'll know. A big fast boat like that would not go unnoticed." She reaches for the phone, but Bob stops her.

"Lets not, yet."

"Bob," she says patiently in that tone which, when she uses it on me, means I probably did something stupid. "I'm not going to ask them about the boat. I'm simply going to check if donuts were delivered this morning. If that boat was launched here, they'll tell me. I won't have to ask."

"Okay."

We both listen. Me, because I'm curious. Why would you launch a cigarette? Cigarettes are stinky things covered by paper. Not boats. But now she's calling it a boat. And Bob agrees that it's a boat.

She asks about donuts and then listens nodding her head with a big smile to Bob. She makes a few comments and hangs up.

"Yep. A red go-fast Cigarette boat. It was a circus. Everyone went out to watch. First they couldn't back the trailer and then they drove the boat off the trailer and crashed into a piling."

Bob frowns and Boston says, "We don't know for sure they're doing anything wrong."

"We don't. But we have guts for a reason. Go-fast here generally means drugs."

"You don't know they have drugs," Boston says.

"A Cigarette? In Flamingo? A big boat like that in Florida Bay? If they were innocent, they'd be out there in the bay, aground." He nods toward the water past the tent camping.

"Maybe they're just fishing in the gulf. It's happened. Remember that go-fast last year?"

"Yeah. They never even got out of sight of the visitor center before they ran aground. Missed the channel marker. I towed them off the mudflat. Tyro boaters, novices. Didn't know a bow from a bow-wow. And they had kids. No idea what they were doing or where they were going. These guys?" He shrugs. "These dudes are wrong, Fey. Remember? You told me."

She puts her fingertips to her temples. "And because I'm fey, I see them meeting a mother boat. Picking up drugs. Heroin? Fentanyl?"

He nods. "Would think so. But we don't know that. Give me a minute." He paces around the kiosk. That's about ten steps. "We're going to keep an eye on these people."

The phone rings and he grabs it. "What? He isn't there? He heading back here? Gone to town? Why would he go to town?" Bob rubs his forehead. "A meeting. The Chief went to that meeting too? Anyone there in authority? You?" He pauses a beat. "Well I might need a few guys. Someone off duty. Later, if things go the way I think. Let me get back to you when I know some more." He disconnects, crumples a piece of paper and tosses it to me. I bat it twice.

"We're on our own. You don't have to worry about Catfish catching Tiger at work. He's in town. Tell me more about the camper."

"He wanted to go through the campground farther south to the water. Told him there was no access back there. Then he wanted to park in the walk-in by the shore. I explained it was a walk-in tent area, no vehicles allowed. No driving on the grass. Told him he could walk to the water's edge. He didn't like it and argued, wanted to pull his boat out of the water there. Must have left his trailer somewhere else, he wasn't towing it."

She takes a breath. "I gave him the spiel. Your boat won't float out there. The water is too shallow. Flats out one hundred yards. Had to explain flats to him." Boston shakes her head. "The woman said they wanted to park by the water. So, I repeated everything. Said if they wanted to park by the water, they should go back to the marina. If they were going to be here overnight, they would have to be in the campground. She said they weren't going to be here overnight."

Boston strokes me one time. "They're wrong Bob. Just a feeling."

Bob nods. "Agree. Okay. We're going to watch and wait." He picks up the phone again.

I nudge Boston for another snack. "Okay kitty. I'll give you a snack." She sets a few treats on the counter.

Yea.

"Kev," Bob says into the phone. "I want to borrow your camper and that wrecked boat you guys towed to the maintenance yard, the moldy sunk boat on the trailer?" He explains what's happening.

"Can Jackson come and get it?"

He listens for a minute. "That's great. It will work better if you go with him. I'm shorthanded right now. I'll have him meet you at your quarters. No uniforms. Go to the Florida Bay ramp. You can be trying to start the boat. Three or four kibitzers on the bench offering advice. I'll get some rangers from the other end to do that."

Bob hangs up, holds up a finger to Boston and dials

again. "Jackson. Meet Kev at his quarters, you're going to hang out at the boat ramp. He'll explain."

He does the disconnect and dial thing again, his fingers moving too quickly for me to pounce. He tells the entrance station he needs backup in Flamingo. Maybe he has something, Maybe not. Then he stares at Boston doubtfully a moment with his lips pressed tight. Makes a decision. "Doug is sending three cars and all the off-duty Rangers. Meanwhile, I want to know how many people are in the truck. In the camper. Descriptions. I don't want to go back down there in the squad car. I need someone to walk out there, sit at a picnic table. Take pictures or sketch. Keep an eye on those men."

"I can do that," Boston says.

"Okay. Watch them. Don't interact with them. You're just a tourist. Put that shirt on." He points to a plaid shirt in the lost and found basket.

"No way I'm putting that on. I'm wearing a T-shirt. I'll just take off my uniform shirt. That will be disguise enough."

"Okay. Just so you don't look like a ranger. Lock up. Tiger is good cover. Take him. Take the golf cart, it's unmarked. Watch them. Sit at a picnic table and sketch. Take pictures. Play with your cell phone. Don't do anything else. If they leave, let me know."

"You think I'm going to jump them or something? I'll sit and watch. I have to finish my ghost orchid sketch. I'll take pictures. Pat the cat."

"Okay. Be careful," he says and, looking all around, he sneaks out the door.

She pulls off her shirt and her scrunchie and shakes out her hair. "Come on, Tiger, get in your case."

Don't really want to get in there, but an adventure? May be worth it. And she packed cat treats.

She pushes me in and zips the flap shut with one hand, reaching for her radio with the other, picks up my cage and, with the same stealthy look all around, heads out the door, locking it behind her. I sit in the front seat in the cart beside her, of course there is only the one seat. The cart doesn't go fast, even with the gas pedal pressed to the floorboards, so she can't stop short, I don't have to worry about being tossed in the footwell. It's a slow ride, but we finally reach the amphitheater at the end of the tent camping area. She picks up my cage and walks to a picnic table in a group of sea grape trees.

"Okay, Tiger, wait here."

Sure. I'll stay right here in my cage like a good kitty. Like I have a choice?

I watch her walk to the shore. She doesn't try to pounce on the cattle egret. Just takes pictures. I'd have jumped him. She walks past him and takes pictures of the three stupid pelicans sitting on rotten pilings. Walks back. Still snapping shots. Of the camper, I think. She sits and opens my door. "You can come out, but you have to wear your leash and no running away. I'll sit here and sketch and take pictures. Now be good and there will be snacks."

A bribe. That works. Not going to run off anyhow.

She snaps the stupid dumb pink yarn leash to my harness. I grimace because the color is embarrassing and look around but there's nothing out here to see. Except the view. The view is boring. Yawn. *Oh.* Something moved. I study the spot. A lizard. On the tree branch. Okay. I walk to the end of the table for a closer look and Boston notices and says, "That's the same type of lizard you tease at home. A green anole, pronounced 'a nol' or 'a nol ee', depending on where you are from. Lizard or chameleon works for me."

Who cares. Doesn't look green.

"It's in its brown phase."

The lizard jumps onto a green sea grape leaf.

And turns green. And almost disappears. Wow. How did that happen?

"There, see," she says. "That is what chameleon means. It can change color to blend with the background. No one can see it."

Hmm. That could be a handy feature. For sneaking up on turkey buzzards or even a roasted turkey. Or if I could blend into a dining room tabletop. That could be cool.

But it hasn't disappeared. I can still see the stupid lizard. And it has a shadow under it.

My eyes go wide when its throat puffs up into a giant red balloon. Huh?

"Kev calls that 'showing his money'. I forget the proper term for that. I'll have to look it up. The lizard puffs up the flap of skin in his throat, dewlap it's called, to defend its territory. Or scare away predators. Like you."

Weird. Dumb thing. First it turns green to blend and hide, then it flashes its throat like a beacon saying, look at me, look at me. Dumb no!. *Silly.* Besides, why would a lizard think that by turning red he'd be able to scare a Maine Coon cat?

Wonder if my throat would puff up into a red balloon? Dumb thing to do. Stupid. Don't want to cam ee lion or change colors.

"People and cats can't change color," Boston says, reading my thoughts.

Bummer. Oh well, can't see any reason I'd want to turn green and look like a leaf. Once I caught a lizard by slamming my paw down on its tail and when I reached down to bite his head, he dropped his tail and ran off. Stupid tail was wiggling back and forth under my paw. Boston told me they do that. Drop off their tails. Stupid. I wouldn't leave my tail behind.

Should I catch him? I wouldn't eat him. Those lizards, a nols, make me sick. They eat bugs. Yuk. I could jump up in the tree and get the stupid lizard. Too much effort. Not that bored and I'm tired and this spot in the sun is fine for a short nap, so I curl up. Listen with one ear as Boston talks to Bob on her cell. "Two people in the camper, one in the truck. They're talking. By the camper. On a cell phone. Looks like they have omni directional booster antennas attached to the camper and truck. Oh, they're all getting into the truck. Wait. They're driving toward us." She holds her breath, a hand on me. "Past us. They drove past us, down to the shoreline. Parking. They are getting out. Looking over the water. Waiting?"

"Stay where you are. Don't do anything. I'm sending backup," Bob says.

"Not going anywhere," she mumbles. "What's he think I'm going to do?" She pulls out her color pencils and starts sketching.

I close my eyes for a nap, but before I can fall asleep, another truck, with a loud engine, pulls up and parks.

Kevlar along with Rangers Jackson and Rose walk by laughing loudly carrying fishing poles and head to the shoreline. Ignore us. Boston whispers that to Bob in her cell. She looks to me and adds, "I'd feel better with more law enforcement guys. On the plus side, maybe they'll catch supper."

Fish supper? My favorite.

A few minutes later, a squad car noses out from the trail behind the motel, hidden from the shoreline. A second car parks behind it. Two more Rangers, in long sleeve flowered shirts, walk to the shore with fishing poles, two stand by the vehicles.

"Pine Island Rangers are on the main park road by the entrance to the campground," Bob says on the cell. "And we have the road blocked at the bridge. If they get by the guys in the campground they're not going anywhere."

"The Rangers have them boxed in, surrounded. Smart," Boston says. "Bob must have decided they're going to try to pull the boat here, now, since it's almost dark. He's pretty sure of himself. Hope they have contraband on board."

Pack hunters. Humans acting like a pack. Didn't know they could do that. Dogs, well wolves, which are just big wild dogs, hunt in packs. Boston says wolves hunt buffalo. Bison they're called, a kind of big wild cow. The buffalo is on the Park Service shield and they live in Yellowstone, a park like here, except instead of a lot of trees and green, Yellowstone has a lot of, well, yellow rocks.

Buzzards kind of work in packs, but that's more like bellying up to the table than hunting. And fire ants just attack. Some cats hunt in packs too. Lions. Not Maine Coon cats, though, we're good hunters, don't need help.

"If those creeps are going to try to pull their boat here,

they are in for a big disappointment. That's skinny water out there. Only six to twelve inches with a mud bottom. Like off the dock at home. Not enough water to float a Cigarette. Pulling that boat here, ain't gonna work, kitty."

Nothing happens so she goes back to her drawing of a ghost orchid, the flower that kind of looks like a white frog jumping up.

Boring. Maybe I do like lizards and hunting seems to be the thing to do. Where is that cam ee lion? Disappeared? Almost miss him, but then the stupid lizard shows his money. I settle into a crouch.

A loud roaring thunder startles me onto my toes. Ready. In defense mode. Attack mode. The roaring echoes over the bay and ends on a high-pitched screech. The distinctive sound of a boat engine which has run out of water and, with its prop digging into the muddy bottom, stops abruptly.

The stupid boat has run aground. A large boat. Sitting there, high and dry. I almost smile. *So there. Startle me will you. Teach you stupid noisy boat.*

Boston gives Bob a play-by-play report. "The two people on board, pick themselves up and yell at each other. They try the engine. Doesn't work. The prop is in the mud and won't turn, won't start. And the water isn't deep enough to float the big boat. They're going to have to get out and walk and they can't walk in the two feet of mud and muck under six inches of water."

Hee hee. This should be fun. Who cares about the stupid lizard.

The two men point angrily at each other and then both climb onto the gunnels. Gunnels has nothing to do with guns. It's a nautical term. Gunnels are the low sides of boats. Used to be, in olden times, Boston said, where the old wooden sailing warships mounted their cannon. Gun wale or gun ridge, I forget which. Oh, gunnels has everything to do with guns.

The men drop into the water. And sink. Tee. Hee. Up

to their waists in water and mud. Gonna' be tough to walk that way.

Tee. Hee. Okay, I'm no longer embarrassed by my pink leash. They flounder. Flounder is another nautical term. It's a fish who hides in the mud.

Jackson and Rose drop their poles and stride over to the three people on the shoreline.

Sirens screaming, one squad car charges out of the trailhead and blocks the truck. Another, from the main road, hurtles through the campground to block the camper.

When the noise dies down, I hear the putt-putt of a small engine and a flat bottom Jon boat eases into sight. Jon boats float in a couple of inches of water. This one has a small engine mounted on the side and glides over to the Cigarette. A Ranger Boston Whaler stops in the channel. A ranger steps onto the bow with a long gun, standing on guard.

Pack hunters Who knew.

"Tiger, those crooks aren't even going to try to run. The ones in the water can't even walk. The Rangers will have to pull them into the Jon boat. And really, where would they go? Thirty-eight miles before they even get out of the park and another five before they reach an intersecting road. Bob is a major tactician and a strategist."

Bob comes by. "Jackson says the boat is full to the gunnels with contraband. The men on the boat are already rolling on the guys in the camper and truck, implicating them. Also telling names of higher ups in Miami. We got them. Tell Faye, thanks."

He starts to drive off, stops. "Like the lizard," he yells out the window.

Lizard? My lizard? No, he's looking at her sketch of a lizard on a grape leaf. My lizard is still… Not on the leaf. He's on the tree branch and has turned brown. He rushes forward and snaps up an ant with his tongue.

Huh. I almost step back. He chews it and swallows and climbs further away into the tree.

"Oh," Bob says, "Kev caught two reds. Rose caught a sheepshead. Fish and hush puppies for everyone tonight. I'll bring salad."

Redfish, my favorite. Who cares about the stupid lizard.

TRUCK BOAT CRASH

We're going to town early, the sun barely rising. Quick trip to the vet who is thirty-eight miles down the main park road from Flamingo where we live permanently now. We're not going back to Boston, because we married Kevlar. I call him Kevlar, everyone else calls him Kev.

About the only time I ride in the car anymore is to go to the vet, a lady doctor who always gives me treats. Very nice treats. Boston has advanced first aid and treats my cuts and owies, but she says only the vet can do vaccinations. I'm pretty sure that isn't the same as vacation.

"You always have fun at the vet," Boston says. "She feeds you good snacks. And I want you to behave today. No terrifying her helper, leave him alone."

If he's there, I threaten him. Attack is instinctive and I don't think I can control it. Besides, it's so easy.

"Okay?" she reaches up and nudges me with her hand. "Be on your best behavior."

Well, I don't have a best behavior. Besides it's boring.

I'm riding behind Boston's neck on the seatback where I can look out all the windows. There's always something to see. And, actually, this is the safest place for me. Boston tends to stop without warning and if I'm not braced behind her neck I get tossed forward.

"We'll pull into Nine Mile Pond and see if there's any bird life." She slows and turns off the main park road. The world ends a few feet beyond the shoreline in a fogbank over the flat, smooth, water. A blurred red smudge behind the fog is the rising sun giving the world an eerie purplish glow. It's almost chilly.

"Red sky in the morning, sailors take warning. That's an old saying from up north. Means the weather will turn bad. But down here, I think it means just the opposite, plus good fishing."

A shadowy shape glides through the fog just above the water and disappears off to the side.

Hunh? I jump down on the seat and put my front feet on the dash keeping my eyes on the spot where it vanished. A few moments later, it comes back, closer now, darker. But still shadowy. Only a blurred shape gliding over the surface of the purple water a few feet from the shoreline. It reaches the other end of the pond and disappears into the fog.

"What was that?" Boston whispers, leaning forward. "Spooky."

The shadow breaks out of the fogbank. A bird, floating above the water. Coasting across the surface, its wings spread to the side, still and unmoving. Floating in a soft hazy purple. Silent. Riding on the tip of its lower beak, carving a V-shape through the water.

It reaches the end and soars up and around, comes back for another sweep in front of us.

"Whoa. Picture. Need a picture," Boston whispers again though I'm sure it can't hear us. She raises her cell phone, points it toward the silent bird as it floats past leaving a long thin wake in the water.

"Skimmer, black skimmer," she murmurs.

The bird wheels up into the fog.

"I saw this picture on the cover of an Audubon magazine a long time ago. Purple skimmer floating above the water," she says, "I thought it was fake. The purple color was so unnatural. But there it is."

We wait, but the bird doesn't return.

Boston settles back in her seat. "Wow. What a great

morning. The skimmer is a black tern, Tiger. It's chin, front, belly, and under its wings, is white. Top of head, wings, and back are black. Has orange where its beak meets its head. The lower beak is much longer than the top beak, so the bird can scoop food off the surface of the water. The top beak, mandible, snaps shut when it feels a fish."

Doesn't sound like fun to me. Looks like a tough way to get a meal. And I didn't see it catch anything.

"Skimmers generally feed at night, well dusk, when the air and water are calm and still. This fog means calm and tranquil, perfect for skimmers." She nods to herself and continues. "The skimmer is slick when flying, but he's a weird looking bird on the ground. His beak is so large he looks ungainly. Always seems to me he's going to tumble forward and fall beak first on his face." She checks her cell. "We got great video, Tiger. All in violet."

We drive down the road a couple of miles at an easy pace, but she suddenly slams on the brakes and tosses me hard against the back of her neck. I scrabble to hang on with my claws.

Yup. That's why I ride on the seatback behind her head. I don't like being tossed through the windshield or into the footwell when she stops short. Its undignified.

Stopping like that generally means she's spotted wildlife, but I don't see any.

"Wow. Look at that. Tiger do you see that?"

No deer, no wild cats, no alligators. I twist all around to check the other windows. Nothing. Then I look in the direction her chin is pointing.

Hmm.

Not wildlife. A pickup truck, nose first down in the water in the culvert, standing almost vertical, the rear end sticking up in the air. Tall sawgrass surrounds it. An empty boat trailer is jackknifed behind it, still connected to the hitch on the truck, the back wheels buried in the dirt on the sloping mowed grass bank. The boat? That's wedged up in some trees in a small hammock just past the truck. The bow, (Boston calls the front of a boat the bow), pointing in the air.

"Look at that boat, just hanging about three feet off the ground in the buttonwood hammock. How did that happen? Truck goes off the road, headfirst in the water flipping the boat off and into the trees and jackknifing the boat trailer. Like dominoes?" Boston looks all around. "There should be Rangers all over the place here. The wreck's been here awhile" She shakes her head. "Morning patrol should have reported it. Maybe they're done here."

She pulls out her cell. "No bars." She steps out of the car. "Stay here, Tiger," she says, holding her phone up in the air while walking toward the wreck.

Huh. Like I'm going somewhere with the doors closed and the windows up. Not sure I'd want to be on my own out here in the swamps even if I could get out. Hmm. One window is partway down.

"Got one bar." She takes a few more steps. "Another bar. I'll try." She pushes some buttons. "Doug?" Doug is at the entrance gate. He's dispatch for the park.

"I'm about at The Well on the main park road and there's a boat and truck wrecked here. Do you know about them?" She waits a moment. "No one reported it?" she says.

"Um, A dark red pickup, old GMC. I can't see the tag, its pointing at the sky. I'd have to climb up into the truck to read it. It's towing a trailer, but that tag is buried in the dirt. The boat is in the trees. Its Florida registration number is FL 23456X."

Watching her footing, she pauses near the truck. "I recognize the rig, it belongs to Double E. I don't see him. I'll look around. I can see a turtle, a loggerhead, on the boat. I'll send you a picture." She takes pictures with her cell.

She left me alone. Alone. In a hot car. Well, sure, she left the a/c on, but still. She gets to walk around. Hmmm. She did leave the window open a little. That must mean she doesn't mind if I get out.

It's not open enough to just jump out. Hmph. I stand and grab hold of the top of the window to climb out, but when I put my full weight on it, it comes down just enough that I can scoot out and drop to the ground. And look around.

Yes. Now what? Guess I'll follow her. She shouldn't wander out here by herself. She needs me to keep an eye on her. And there may be a treat. I start toward her across the grass.

Ahhh. What? I'm standing in cold, wet, skinny water and sinking into some spongey stuff. Green spongy grass. Wet, cold, green, spongy.

Yuk. She didn't tell me it was wet. That's why she was walking funny, watching her feet. I back up to dry land. Firm, dry land. Everything in front of me is covered with water. As far as I can see, grass growing out of water. Boston has told me about the water in the swamps, I just never understood.

Little tiny fish swirl in the water and I reach out and

tap the surface. They scatter. Wow. But now my paw is wet again. I shake it and lick it dry.

Boston's talking into her cell. "I don't see Double E. He must have caught a ride. Maybe went for help and will come back for his boat and truck. Maybe the District Ranger gave him a lift when he did his early morning road patrol." She's standing on tiptoe to see in the truck.

I sniff. Tilt my head and sniff again. Blood. And sweat. And sick. *Yuk*. I follow my nose, staying on the dry short mown grass. Not going in that wet stuff again.

"Hey," Boston yells. "You're supposed to be in the car. Come here. Stay out of the road. Don't go into the swamp." She hollers all those instructions as she comes cautiously toward me. She probably thinks I'm going to run off and play catch-me.

Me? Another time, I might. But I stare at the man.

"You see something Tiger?" She walks two steps closer.

I imagine myself rolling my eyes. *Yeah, I see something.*

"Oh, Double E. You found him. He's bloody. Is he dead? Tell me he's not dead. I don't want to come any closer if he's dead."

Really? She's doesn't want to check the guy out? She has all that training. And she has a bunch of books on cat injuries and illnesses and doctors me.

"I can be brave." She stands tall, straightens her shoulders. "You stay where you are. I don't have time to chase you." She edges slowly past me toward the guy in the grass and stops. Hesitates.

"I have to check him. This is what I've trained for, all

those first aid, CPR, emergency medical classes. But I didn't actually ever intend to touch a dead person. Or one bleeding. Argh. I never intended to be first man on the scene. Always planned to be the back-up, go-for guy." She looks around desperately, but it's only her and me. She takes a cautious step toward the man. Looks closely and exhales.

"He's breathing. That's good."

She clicks her cell. "Douglas, you better send the ambulance, too. Tiger just found Double E, Edgar Evans. I'll check him for vitals and call in his status as soon as I get it. I haven't found his buddy Warren, they're generally together. He could have walked. Or maybe EE was alone."

She runs back to the car, grabs her first aid kit, and trots over to the guy. "I sounded professional, didn't I? Like I know what I'm doing? My voice didn't crack did it?" She stoops down. "I really, really don't want to do this." She prods and presses. Touching gently all over. The same way she does me.

She stops and looks at me.

"Oh, no. I told him you found Double E. We're both going to be in trouble. I don't suppose you would get back into the car by yourself?" She looks at me.

No. I don't suppose so either.

Double E groans and she pulls her hands back in surprise. "Buck up girl," she says to herself. "That's a good sign." She continues examining him. "Hey, I can do this. Who'd a thought?"

She seems to have forgotten me and something is moving

in the tall grasses in the water, rustling. I creep over, staying on solid land.

Boston puts her cell on speaker. "Douglas. Ready to copy vitals?" she asks and when he replies affirmative, she reads off numbers. "Nothing critical. Gashes and cuts. No broken bones, except ribs maybe, so I don't need to splint anything. Nothing we can do about the ribs."

She tried to splint my leg once. For practice. It didn't work out very well.

"You know Double E almost always travels with Warren," she tells the dispatcher again. "Can't think of his last name just now. Anyone report a lone man on the road this morning?"

"Nothing," the entrance station says.

"Might want to send out a patrol to look for him."

"Already dispatched him." And the park radio in the car squawks, a ranger saying he's on his way.

More rustling. In the tall grass, sawgrass. Sawgrass is tough. Boston brought some home once after a tourist pulled it up and sliced his hand. She was going to replant it. She'd pushed my paw away when I tried to grab it and told me, "Sawgrass has saw-like teeth along its edge, it is sharp. It's not really a grass. It's a sedge."

I'm not sure what a sedge is, but it looks like grass and something is moving cautiously in the sedge.

I point my ears toward the sound. A long yellow beak pokes out followed by a white head, a bird. His head sways to the left and a long white neck appears. A tall bird. I can see a white body and long yellow legs in the grasses. White heron. Or, as Boston said when this bird tried to terrify me when we first moved here, a great blue heron in its white phase.

Looks like a white bird to me.

Doesn't even notice me, but it is coming in my direction with each step. A white bird with a problem. His head is tilted sideways. He straightens his head and it flops slowly over onto the other side. He edges a tad more out of the grasses. His head flips over again. One eye pointed in the water. He must be having a spasm.

Or is he hunting? He could be looking in the water.

Slowly, he edges through the sedges.

Oh boy. A tad closer and he'll be in pouncing range. He'll still be in the water, but it's shallow. I'll get my feet wet, but once I have him down, I can drag him out to dry land pretty quick.

I sink down low on my belly, squint my eyes, flick my tail. Cackle. *Oops*. Didn't mean to cackle. It just came out. But he didn't hear.

Boston does hear and looks over. Points a finger at me. "Leave it alone," she says and goes back to treating the Double E guy.

Don't think so.

I track the bird while she talks. Spare her a quick glance as she wipes some blood off the guy's head. "You know, Tiger, I always wondered about these two guys. A little too slick. A little too nervous. Edgy. Strange behavior for guys who are just going fishing. Looks like they've been poaching the wildlife."

She asks the entrance station, "What's ETA on the ambulance?"

"Bob's enroute from Flamingo, ten minutes. The District Ranger will be right behind him."

"Just my luck," she says. "Catfish is coming. You need to get back in the car, Tiger. Come here."

I twitch an ear at her, watching the bird move closer. One more step. I flatten my ears, wiggle my butt, tense my muscles. The bird freezes a moment. Stabs the water. Jerks its head up and around, points his break, full of a silvery fish, to the sky.

Hunh? Kind of like the reddish egret we watched on Thanksgiving, except this is a much larger fish.

The bird shakes his head and I step back.

It flips the fish into the air, catches it and swallows it down headfirst.

Whoa. I back up a few more steps.

Right into Boston's waiting hands. *Oops.* While I was watching the bird swallow the fish, she'd snuck up on me.

Stupid bird.

"I'll give you a treat in the car." She holds me firmly and gets in the car with me. Reaches in her pocket and pulls out a packet of cat snacks. "Trout Treats." She shakes the bag and offers me one.

Well, why not. I take a kernel gently out of her hand. She drops a half dozen treats on the seat and rolls the window up. All the way.

Bummer.

"Stay here now. If Catfish sees you out on your own, he'll probably shoot you. I better turn off the radio, too. Don't want him to know I carry one to town." She turns it off and covers it with a towel. "Double E is doing okay. He can talk. I think he has some cracked ribs. I'll let the EMTs decide if he needs strapping. I made him comfortable." She sidles out of the car.

I eat my treats keeping an eye on her. Dangerous birds out there. She picks her way around the truck peeking into the bed and snapping pictures. "Turtles," she says to herself. "Two loggerheads, protected. Still alive at least." She looks in the open front door. "Airbag deployed. Small amount of blood on the front seat." She leans over and snaps more pictures. Looks behind the seat. "Humph. Two rifles in back here." She faces the boat. "Coolers tipped and busted open. At least two short out-of-season snook."

I hear a siren now, screaming. It gets louder and the ambulance screeches to a stop. The door opens and Bob steps out staring at the wreck. He whistles. "That's been here a while." Jackson gets out the passenger door.

"Double E is over here," she tells him and leads him over. "I was afraid you were Catfish."

Bob guffaws. "He'll be here soon. He had the early morning road patrol. If he'd done it, he'd have seen this wreck. Hard to miss. Idiot." He gave the wreck another look. "Obvious it happened hours ago. How's Double E doing?"

"Check him out. My first time as first on scene."

He stoops over the guy.

"Hey, EE? How you doing man?"

Double E groans.

Bob shakes his head and checks EE's pulse himself, then looks closely at the head wound. "You did a good job," he tells Boston. "The hospital can clean the rest of the blood off, don't want to start fresh bleeding. Eyes are okay, so no head injury. Can't do anything about the ribs." He nods again. "Good job, Mrs. First Responder."

Boston beams at him.

A squad car screams up and Catfish jumps out screaming like the siren. "You check that man. She's not an EMT. Make sure she didn't do any harm," he orders Bob. "And you," he hollers to her, "you touch that boat? You touch that truck? You're in big trouble if you did." His warning to her is meant to be blistering, but his voice breaks and he sounds like a girl.

I growl from my spot on the seat. Maybe the bird will get him.

"Nope. Didn't," Boston replies with restraint.

"You had to, how else would you know there's turtles in them," he says.

"Walk around the trailer, you can see inside the truck bed," she tells him and turns her back on him but watches over her shoulder. Then, when he starts around the trailer she says, quickly, "Not that way, go around my car to the other side."

"Don't try to tell me what to do," he yells. "I said to check the guy. She's not an EMT," Catfish stomps toward the trailer and tromps into knee deep water before he even realizes it. He swears.

Heh, heh. Cats can laugh.

Bob says quietly to Boston, "Ignore him. His Little Napoleon complex is showing."

"Yeah." They share a quiet laugh.

Kevlar calls in. "I just found Warren. He's okay. Drunk, by the smell of him, and passed out on a picnic table at Paurotis Pond. Been here awhile. Still got dew on him. Send the ambulance for him after you load Double E."

Catfish turns and trudges to dry land, stepping high, but sinking into that spongy stuff.

Boston sucks in her cheeks. Bob frowns.

Catfish yells at Bob. "Go check out the boat. See if there are any animals or plants."

Boston says, "Go on the other side of my car, Bob. The

water is shallower. And you can look inside the truck too. I got pictures on my cell. I sent them to dispatch."

"Thanks," he whispers to her.

Catfish pulls out his radio and calls the entrance station, "I'm on scene," he says, only to hear them reply, "Chief Ranger wants you in his office."

He smirks. "Yeah, when I finish here."

"No, he said to tell you to head up now. Leave Bob in charge there."

Catfish grins and says importantly, "You heard him. They need me at headquarters. You're in charge for a while. Be sure and have this guy taken to the hospital. Get these wrecks moved out of here. Don't mess up." He struts to his vehicle, wet feet and all, pulls out into the road siren wailing.

Bob's shakes his head, hands on his hips. "Wonder if he thinks I'm going to forget to send Double E to the hospital."

"Yeah, we wouldn't want that to happen. Have him still be here when Catfish comes back up the road," she says that in an amused tone. "Though, I wouldn't be surprised if the boat is still in the trees."

"He should have noticed this wreck. Would have, if he'd done patrol. I wondered when the schedule came out and saw he'd put himself in for the early morning road patrol. I've seen the squad car in the residence parking lot every morning this week, hoped he'd been up the road and had come back for some coffee. The man doesn't even roll out of bed 'til nine and always comes in late"

"You think the Chief knows that?"

"Oh, yeah. I'll bet he checked the schedule as soon as you called this wreck in."

"Catfish will probably have a good excuse."

Bob keys his radio. "Kev? Jackson and I'll pick up Double E first and then come get Warren, you copy?"

"Got it," Kevlar responds.

"Then can you come here and let me know if we can manage the removal of the wrecks ourselves or if we need to call in a local wrecker?"

"Ten-four."

"We have to go," Boston says.

"We?"

"I have Tiger, he's going to the vet." She heads back to the car and he follows and bends down to say hi.

Boston says, "He found Double E."

"Oh, won't Catfish just love that if it shows up in a report."

"I think it might. I slipped and told dispatch." Boston laughs. "Want my pictures?"

Two squad cars pull in from headquarters. "Yeah, please. And I'll have these guys get more before we disturb the scene."

He leans down and says, "Have fun, Tiger."

"He will. He likes to terrify the vet's assistant."

I raise my head proudly.

"Sorry, I'm going to miss that. It's always an adventure when I take Wolf in. Sometimes I think I should just drug him first."

Stupid cat should be drugged. Better not drug me.

The rest of our trip is uneventful and Boston parks at the vet. She carries me inside into an atmosphere of nervous fear. Can't imagine why. I always have such fun. One dog is woofing, and two others are sitting by their people shaking. Trembling. It's sad. The only cat has his head hidden. And the bird sitting on that man's shoulder, pooping down his back, is squawking, "Big dog. Big dog."

Eww. He pooped on that guy's shirt and the guy doesn't even care. Yuk.

It's our turn. *Yay. Yummy treats coming up.*

We walk into the room and Boston sets my cage on the table and opens the door. I step out. The table is cold, and my toes curl and my smile turns into a frown of displeasure which I point at the man. The assistant. I kind of smile at him. Lean forward, tail straight up, ears flat along the top of my head, raise my hackles, and snarl. Ferociously

He makes an about face, bumps into the table, drops his clipboard, and flees out of the room.

Hee hee. Hah. Idiot. Tee hee. Oh man, what could be better.

"Tiger Fat Cat," Boston admonishes me. "Bad cat."

Well, the words admonish; the tone is proud. I preen a little. Sit and clean my paw, giggling inside. *Tee hee.* That was fun. The guy is too easy.

"Bad cat. You are so bad. What am I going to do with you?"

I work on my paw cleaning until the pretty lady comes in and repeat my terrorizing performance.

She just laughs at me. "Treat?"

Well, yeah, that's why I'm here. I sit in my ready for treat now position.

She holds out a beef chip. My favorite.

"What did you do to my assistant?"

I blink my eyes innocently. She gives me the chip and I eat it delicately.

"I have chicken and salmon treats in my pocket here. Let's see how you do."

She touches me all over. Boston keeps hold of me as the vet runs her hands down my sides, over my front legs. A lot like Boston just did with Double E. Kind of tickles.

The lady fools me with the mouth thing by squeezing my jaw so my mouth opens. She looks inside quick.

I can't reach up to push her hand away because Boston has a tight grip on my front legs. I start a snarl, but the doctor drops a treat in. Salmon. My favorite. While I'm busy chewing it, she stabs my butt.

What? I spin around and open my mouth to complain and she pops in another treat.

Chicken. My favorite.

She gives me another treat before I can swallow this one. Turkey. Cool. My favorite. She drops two more treats on the table and tells Boston what a wonderful healthy cat I am.

Huh. Not just a cat, lady, but a Maine Coon cat. Strong, valiant, brave. Even though I don't have the tufted ears.

Boston pushes me toward the extra treats in my cage, zips me up, and we head back after a successful fun visit. Don't know why those other animals are so afraid.

Truck Boat Crash

We stop at the wreck.

"The town wrecker got the trailer first, then pulled the truck out of the culvert," Bob says. "The boat presented problems and we had to bring in the aire-lift." He points to the metal contraption which raises up into the air on a long arm. It reaches over and grabs the boat with metal teeth and lifts it out of the trees, then carries the boat to the flatbed trailer and places it behind the boat trailer.

Boston says, "Double E is going to have a big bill. Those grapple arms are not cheap. How's he doing?"

"They're going to keep him overnight at the hospital and then he'll join Warren in jail. Protected turtles, undersize, out-of-season, fish. We found a couple of air plants. They'll both get hefty fines. Maybe some real prison time for being stupid. Drunk and stupid. Almost feel sorry for the two of them. But I'm too angry at the thought that they've been doing this under our noses."

"What about Catfish?"

Bob laughs. "He'll be working out of the Chief Ranger's Office for the next month."

I eat my last crunchie and settle down for a nap. Time to go home.

BLACK OLIVES

Boston's voice slips into my dreams.

"Let me tell you about this sweet little angel," she says. "This mischievous imp has been a tornado of destruction today."

Me? Is she talking about me? Hey. I worked hard. I half open an eye.

"First, the spare room. He knocked all the painted rocks off the table."

My lip twitches. I did that. One at a time. It was fun.

"I picked them up."

She likes to pick up after me. After I knocked the rocks off, a crow landed on the ledge outside and I tried to get him, but...

"He'd also snapped the shade cord, so it was wrapped around the curtain rod. I fixed that and noticed the window had dirty cat paw and nose prints all over it. Looked out through the prints and saw three bullets on the windowsill."

"Bullets?" Kevlar asks his head tilted. A frown on his face.

"Right. Bullets. On the windowsill. Three of them. While I was puzzling it out, a fish crow landed with a ring in his beak. He dropped it alongside the bullets and laughed like they do. Ha, ha. Ha, ha."

"Crows will do that," Kevlar says. "Pick up anything shiny. Bullets, watches, rings."

"I added my fingerprints to Tiger's prints, tapped on the window to chase him off. He wasn't fazed, so I opened the window and swiped at him. He flew off complaining loudly."

"Wonder who owns the bullets. The ring." Kevlar says.

"The ring was engraved. The new guy. His initials. I called him and asked if he was missing his ring. And he yelled into the phone that some huge black bird stole his ring. Just swooped down, grabbed it, and flew off. I calmed him down and made him listen while I patiently explained about fish crows and their habit of picking up anything shiny and carrying it off. Guy didn't even know about the bullets. I told him he could come on by and get his stuff, I'd be home all morning."

She pokes me gently. "Yes. Home all morning, chasing around cleaning up after this Whirling Dervish of a cat."

Huh? I was working.

"Next, I caught Tiger on the deck digging in the plants. Your tomato starters. Didn't touch the peppers, onions, or herbs."

"I think some mint seeds got mixed up with the tomatoes. They smell like catnip."

"Anyhow, when I chased him off, he tracked dirt through the house and by the time I caught up with him, he'd been in the clean clothes I left on the couch."

Playing with my catnip mouse.

"I sorted those and put the ones with your plant dirt back in the washer. Then I went into the office to print out a party notice and found he'd been in there ahead of me. He'd been up on the desk and knocked a pile of paperclips off, followed those with two pencils. He scratched through your printouts, leaving little tears. Then, I guess he laid down on top of a second pile of your papers and took a nap on top of them, leaving more dirt specks."

Did not nap. Curled up maybe for a few minutes. I was working.

"I picked up the paperclips and pencils and reprinted the torn papers for you. You can check and see if you need to reprint the ones he slept on."

She kind of bops me on the head. "Let me see. Um. By that time my rewashed laundry was done, and I carried it into the bedroom to fold and put away. That's when the new guy came for his bullets. I advised him not to leave shiny things outdoors. He said he had only turned away for a second to eat a cookie. I mentioned that crows like food too."

"Crows steal everything. Got half my sandwich one day. Stole it right out from in front of me when I was distracted. Flew off with it."

A bird stole Kevlar's sandwich? And lived? He sounds sad. I would be too, if a crow got my lunch.

"I close my eyes and I can see him flying off with my roast beef sandwich, still in its baggie, hanging in his talons," he grumbles. "Guess they don't know they're supposed to eat bugs and snails, carrion and seeds. Not my sandwich."

She laughs. "I saw one pick up a stick and poke it in a hole for a bug. Where was I? What number am I up to? Doesn't matter. When I came back to the bedroom, Tiger had pulled my freshly laundered uniform shirt out of the laundry basket and dragged it off the bed. What did he want with my shirt?"

Smelled good.

"I leaned over to pick it up and saw he'd also pulled the afghan down there too. It was rolled up in a corner. Why would he do that?"

"He's your cat. Why are you asking me?" Kevlar says.
It had tassels and I was playing with those.
"For some reason it was covered with dust bunnies."
Dust bunnies? I didn't see any bunnies. I almost lift my head
"I had to hand pick them off. That stuff really sticks."
Kevlar's laugh almost wakes me completely up. I peek at him, in that half-asleep zone. "Dust bunnies in our house? No way," he says making it sound like there are lots of bunnies in the house. Maybe when I get up, I'll go look for them.

"I don't want to hear about my poor dusting. Or mopping, as the case may be. Someday I'm going to discover a way to knit dust into a blanket. Don't get me sidetracked. I'm still trailing the cat around the house. Where was I? Oh. After I cleaned the quilt and put the clothes away, I went looking for him. Too quiet, you know. I found him in the closet chewing the shoelaces on your boating shoes."

They weren't very good. Didn't have any taste and they were tough.
"I stopped him before he chewed through them, but they're kind of soggy. I shooed him out of the closet, and I was putting your shoes on the shelf to dry, when I heard this horrific scream. Long unending cat wail. My heart stopped." She moves one hand gently over me.

"While I was still frozen, Tiger came charging into the room. Dashing, leaping, thrashing, growling, howling.

I thought he was having a fit. Lashing his tail. Something was on it. He leapt up onto the bed, off the bed, around the bed, rolled in a ball. Jumped up. He was screaming and whipping his tail through the air, twirling it. A piece of my duct tape was stuck to the tip of his tail."

She stops and strokes me again. "I almost laughed in relief."

Laughed? She almost laughed?

"He howled. Hurtled out of the room. I chased him out, around the living room, down the hall. Him shrieking. Me shrieking. Like a couple of loons."

*I was running from that mean thing that had my tail. S*he was charging after me screaming and yelling Stop! Tiger! Stop! Tiger! It was scary. And that thing on my tail wouldn't let go. It attacked me for no reason. Reached out and grabbed my tail. Wouldn't let go. I raced away. Tried to outrun it. It hung on. I couldn't shake it. It clung to my tail. I ran down the hall. Twisted into the living room. It still hung on. I couldn't shake it off. Then the other end brushed my back. I raced back toward Boston and she reached out, but the thing whipped by my head. It was pulling my fur and making a whooshing noise flapping behind me. I raced around the bed, into the bathroom yelling, *Grab it. Grab it. Pull it off. Ow, ow. Let go, let go. Get it off. Get it off. Get it off*

"I finally managed to trap him in the bathroom when he rolled over and tried to grab the tape."

She strokes my head. "Poor thing. I don't know which one of us was more frightened. Both our hearts were pounding. Hindsight, it's kind of funny."

Was not. It was terrifying until she caught me and lifted me into the air. Held me close. Pulled the thing off my tail. It was awful.

"Poor kitty," she says. She pats my tail gently and lifts up the tip. "See. I pulled some fur off removing the tape. He has a naked spot. I had to calm him down, he was frantic. I gave him some tuna."

"Of course, you did," Kevlar says dryly.

Yeah, the tuna was good. And maybe I should get more tuna.

"I was exhausted," Boston says. "I pulled him into my lap and we both napped on the rocking chair in the bedroom."

Well I was tired. And her lap was warm and comforting. And safe.

"Huh," Kevlar says. "That's a lot for one day, even for Tiger. I think we should keep him away from duct tape."

"Good idea. There should be a warning label advising cats to stay clear of duct tape. He was a Whirling Dervish, though I'm not even sure what a Whirling Dervish is. My Granny used to call us kids that when we raced mindlessly around."

"I can tell you."

"No kidding. What?"

"An order of Muslim clerics practice whirling as a religious dance. Whirling Dervish. The dance is performed to express emotion and achieve the wisdom and love of God. It's a very sacred and secret Islamic tradition in Turkey. Actors put on Whirling Dervish performances."

"Huh. How do you know about it?" Boston asks.

"Gail told me. She visited Turkey with Jane. Janet also told me she saw them."

"Weird. I mean weird that my Granny should know about it."

Boston strokes me again. "So Whirling Dervish to sleeping beauty. That was my day."

I continue my nap as they wander out of the room.

Hunh? What's that?

I stick my nose up in the air. Sniff. Not catnip. Sniff. Sniff. No. Not catnip. But sort of catnip. Sniff. Wetter than catnip. Fresher.

The scent is coming from the dining room.

Nap is definitely over and I roll to my feet and follow my nose down the hall.

Hmm. Now I smell popcorn too. I like popcorn. Well not the hard kernels, I leave those. But I like the buttery, salty, soft outsides. Boston shares. Grudgingly. Kevlar doesn't eat it, so more for us. Me.

They are sitting together at the table.

Sniff? The wet catnip is gone. Sniff. Only a leftover trace remains. Where did it go? I still smell popcorn and butter. That's good. I can see it on the table in front of Boston and jump into her lap, but she moves it out of my reach.

"Merow," I say, sweetly, pointing with my nose.

I can be nice.

"You want some popcorn, Sweetie?" she asks. "Let me pick you out a nice piece."

Well, I could pick it out myself. I would have to lick three or four others first. But I guess she knows that.

I take the chosen piece gently from her hand. All salt and butter. Nothing better. Drop it on her leg and scooch down to lick it.

"No, Tiger. I didn't mean for you to smear butter all over my pant leg," she squawks.

I'll lick it clean.

She holds me still by the shoulders and slips a napkin under my kernel. When she releases me, I take a moment to glare up at her and go back to licking delicately.

Yummy. I lick all the butter off first. The best part. Then chew the soft part. Swallow. Look over for more.

She passes me another.

"Make yourself at home, Tiger, why don't you," Kevlar says with a laugh.

"He did," Boston grumbles.

"That's the truth. Interesting. The two of you bonding over an excuse to eat butter and salt."

"He's kind of cute," she says in that tone that means she's proud of me and she runs a hand down my back.

Kevlar picks up a jar and twists the lid, opening it with a click.

I stop mid-lick.

Wet catnip. Open my mouth. Breathe in the amazing heady sweet smell. Close my eyes, savoring.

Who cares about salt and butter?

I get up. Step on his leg, closer to the jar.

He jerks.

I jump into his lap and he kind of screeches and lurches back. Raises both arms up by his head. The jar in the farthest hand. His muscles all tighten under my feet. *Cool.*

"What? What's he doing in my lap? He never jumps in my lap."

Mine. Gimme.

I can't reach the hand with the jar. I start to climb across his chest. But he lowers his other hand and blocks me and squeaks, "Stop him. Help me. Why is he climbing up me?"

Boston leans in toward me. "I think he wants your black olives."

Blackolives? Is that what the scent is? *Mine.*

I squeeze under his arm, and continue my climb up his chest, aiming for the jar.

He blocks me again. His blackolive hand moving farther away. "What? You want the olives? She's right? You want a black olive?"

Yes, I want a blackolive. Smart man.

"You don't want the olives. Cats don't eat olives," he declares still holding it out of reach.

Yes. I do. I want whatever is in that jar.

My mouth is watering.

Boston says, "He wants the olives. Give him an olive."

I sink a couple of claws through his shirt. Leap up, grasp his wrist with both paws and tug his hand.

"Ow," he screams. "Okay then. Okay. Get off me. Go ahead. Look." He shoves the open jar toward my nose. "You'll see you don't want them."

I know what I want. I hook both paws around the jar. Clutching it to me so he can't pull it away. Inhale the aroma. The fragrance makes me a little dizzy. Stick my head in. Reach my tongue down for a taste. The tip just reaches the liquid. Pull it back in and savor the flavor.

Oh, yes. This is the best ever.

Heaven.

"It's people food, Tiger." Boston says. "Kev is right. Cats don't eat olives."

Yes they do. I try to tilt the jar to reach the blackolives. Kevlar pulls it away.

"GRRR." I start after it.

Boston reaches between the two of us, puts the cap on the jar and twists it closed.

What? Gone? Why? The sweet aroma is gone, leaving a faint fragrance. But I'm a Maine Coon cat and we're not dumb. I sit on my haunches and stare at the jar. Willing it open.

"Are you okay for a minute," she asks Kevlar. "While I check online? See if cats can eat olives? Black olives?"

"You don't think he'll claw me do you," Kevlar asks anxiously.

"Nah. Maybe. A minute."

I dig in my back claws. Just a little. He moves the jar and I follow the motion with my eyes.

Boston says, "Cats can eat black olives. The olives have a chemical which affects some cats like catnip."

Yes. Like catnip. Only better than catnip. Way better than catnip. Even better than fresh catnip which I don't get very often.

Mostly the catnip comes wrapped in a cloth mouse which I lick. I don't get to eat it.

"Some cats like them," she says. "I'd say Tiger is one of them. So I guess it would be okay to give him one. Here, I'll open it."

She does, and I move toward the jar.

Kevlar blocks me again. "Just hold on, I'll get you an olive. Settle down. Crazy cat." He reaches in with two fingers and pulls out a shiny dripping black globe.

I pounce. Knock it out of his hand. It falls on the floor and rolls. I jump after it. Grab it. Lick it all over.

"Great. Now I get to clean the floor," Boston says. With that proud smile in her voice.

Yum. Yummy. I try to bite off a piece, but it rolls, won't stay still.

Swallow it whole. Gulp. All gone.

More. I come back to Kevlar and look at the jar. *One more.*

"What do you think?" he asks Boston. "Another?"

"I guess, he knows what's good for him. I hope."

I do. I do. Though I'm feeling just a little dizzy.

Kevlar holds out another.

Boston's still reading on her tablet. "The chemical makes some cats drunk. Which I expect explains why Tiger acts like he's bonkers. Is he stoned?"

Am not. My eyes don't need to open all the way. I finish this second olive and look around toward the jar again.

"Wait," Boston says. "We should probably cut him off until we see what the effects are. He looks tipsy."

"He'll attack."

For sure. Mine.

"Hmm. I have an idea." She passes him an old catnip mouse. "Take this and drip some juice on it and toss it to him."

I watch closely. Not too sure about this. Catnip mouse in blackolive juice? But I pounce on the mouse when he tosses it on the floor. *Yes. Yes.* Lick it once. Rub my cheek on it, my sensor whiskers. Even better.

"I think he's drunk," Boston says.

I'm distracted by a large rat by the door. Charge it. Tackle it.

"Hey, that's my dress shoe," Kevlar hollers.

It is a strange rat. Smells a lot like Kevlar's shoe and doesn't have a tail.

I try to stand but can't get my legs under me, so I bite

the rat lying down and roll around with it and scratch it with my hind legs until it's dead and not moving. The slaughter exhausts me. With one paw over the dead rat, I put my head down and close my eyes. And dream of hunting a herd of large-eared orange rats.

Visions of pizza dance into my dreams and mix with orange rat heads. I wake up with my head on Kevlar's stinky shoe. *Yuk.*

Pizza? I smell pizza? Do I smell pizza? I might be able to open an eye for pizza. I try. My nose catches a better whiff. It is pizza. Ummm. Sniff? Sniff. Pizza with hamburger and sausage. My favorite. It always comes with peppers and onions too, but that's kind of like feathers on birds. You got to pick them off or eat around them. Not that I'd know anything about bird feathers. I don't eat birds.

Wait. They're having pizza? And no one called me. Just let me sleep through it?

Well maybe they did call me, and I didn't hear them, I was dreaming pretty hard slaying that shoe shaped rat.

And blackolives. I smellblackolives. Pizza and blackolives. Two of my most favorite foods. What a wonderful world I live in. Why did I never notice before?

Now both eyes are open wide.

Ohh boy. Blackolives. Yummy. The smell is coming from the living room. I jump up, head down the hall, and peek in.

No one in there. But the fresh pizza smell is coming from here. I check all around and walk in and over to the coffee table. Peek over the edge. Two slices just sitting there all by themselves. With all those wonderful smells.

They must have left these slices for me. Why else would they leave them out where I can reach them?

They must be for me.

I'm allowed on the coffee table. Sort of. Especially if they leave my pizza there. I raise up on my hind legs and look at my slices. I don't see blackolives, but I smell them. My two slices waiting for me.

No one is around.

I jump up. Sniff again. Deep inhale. The blackolives are buried in the cheese and sauce. Not round blackolives, these are sliced. That's good, because the whole round blackolives are hard to eat. Easier to eat this way. I delicately pick one out of the cheese and chew, savor, swallow.

Ooh sooo very very good. Feels good all the way down, warming my tummy, not with heat, but with a warm feeling, comfortable and relaxing.

I snatch another blackolive and chew contentedly. The next one is wedged in tomato sauce, not my favorite. I try it. Chew thoughtfully. Hmm. The sauce isn't too bad. Nothing wrong with a little tomato sauce.

I rub my cheek on the slice. Then the other cheek. The sensors in my whiskers send the scent directly to my brain.

Ooh so good.

I chew my away across the first slice, picking out the blackolives, and then the second slice, chewing, swallowing, wallowing. A little woozy.

Can't find any more.

Sniff all over. They can't all be gone.

Nooo.

I lick the empty spots where the blackolives were, trying to get the last drop. Even lick up the cheese. It's chewy. And the sauce. I lick down to the crust, leaving a dent. Lap anything that remotely smells of blackolive.

All gone. And things get a little bit blurry and muddle my brain.

But hope is not lost. I start eating the chunks of sausage and hamburg. I pick them off, don't leave dents under them.

I'm suddenly laying down. Chin flopped on a pizza slice, my front paws flat out in front of me on either side, protecting it from scavengers.

I squint at a hunk of hamburger. Stick my tongue out

toward it, but it's too far away. I can't lift my head. Too tired after a tough day. I'll get it in a minute. I'll clean my face later too. I can feel the cheese and tomato stuck to it. I'm too tired to deal with it and I can't seem to lift a paw to wipe. A little blackolive scent remains. I smile and fall asleep. And dream of blackolives and butter and pizza.

I hear voices again. Not far away, but kind of fuzzy. Coming closer.

Kevlar says, "What the heck?"

Ooops.

Boston laughs. "Oh, Tiger's fallen asleep, isn't he cute. Our sleeping beauty."

I am.

"He's passed out. And on our pizza," Kevlar points out.

Caught.

"Oh, poor baby. Did the pizza make you tired?" Boston coos and lifts me up with gentle hands.

My head flops down and she puts a supporting arm under it. "He is completely out of it. Looks like he ate some pizza."

"Yeah, my olive and sausage pizza."

"Poor baby has tomato sauce on his face and stuck in his whiskers. Oh, my." She giggles.

Kevlar snorts. "He's licked little holes down through the crust. Must have been where the black olives were, cause they're all gone. Might not have been such a good idea to add the leftover olives to the frozen pizza. Still lots of meat left. And onions and peppers. Guess I could eat around those spots."

No. My pizza.

Kevlar grumbles, "Never seen him do anything like that to pizza. What kind of cat does that?"

"This kind. He is one of those cats who thinks black olives are catnip. Poor kitty. Let me clean your face." I hear rustling and then feel a cool wipe across my cheek. And another. The cloth goes by my nose and I sigh. A quick wisp of olives. *Mmmm.*

"Looks kind of beat," Kevlar says. "Too tired to even flutter an eyelid. Sluggard." Then he says, "I'm still hungry, and he ate my pizza. You could make me some, ah, little Bugle corn chips filled with cream cheese with a black olive on top."

I like cream cheese. And bugles. What's a bugle corn chip?

"Where did you ever get an idea like that?" Boston asks. She sounds a little shocked.

"This guy, One Leg. I told him about Tiger and black olives. He suggested it."

"I wonder how you'd get the cream cheese into the bugle without breaking it."

"You could do it honey."

"Not in this lifetime. How about some peanut butter on toast?"

"Make mine almond butter and I'm with you. Guess I'll leave the slices for him to finish when he wakes up. Nothing like rewarding bad behavior."

I could eat toast. I'm still half asleep. Half dreaming.

But I could wake up for toast. Or hamburger and sausage on pizza. Both.

RAE'S RECIPES

SWEET POTATO SURPRISE
(SOUTHERN LIVING 1984) THIS IS A VERY SWEET DESSERT

6 medium sweet potatoes
1 can vanilla frosting
1 teaspoon vanilla
1 teaspoon almond extract
½ teaspoon ground cinnamon
Optional 1/4 cup coconut
Optional 1 teaspoon almond extract
2 cups mini marshmallows

Boil sweet potatoes, drain, cool, mash
Except for marshmallows add all ingredients
Pour into 9 X 13 pan, uncovered
Bake at 350 degrees for 18 minutes
Layer marshmallows on top and brown in oven.

CURRIED CARROT SOUFFLE
(FAMILY CIRCLE 2012)

Ingredients

2 pounds carrots, peeled and cut into 1/2-inch pieces
1/2 cup sugar
4 tablespoons unsalted butter, melted
3 eggs, beaten
3 tablespoons all-purpose flour
1 tablespoon curry powder
1 teaspoon baking powder
3/4 teaspoon salt

Directions

Heat oven to 350 degrees. In a large, sided saute pan, add carrots. Cover with 1 inch of water and bring to a boil. Reduce heat to medium and cook 12 minutes or until carrots are softened. Drain.

Place carrots in a food processor; process for 30 seconds. Add sugar, butter, eggs, flour, curry powder, baking powder and salt. Process mixture until smooth. Transfer mixture to a buttered 1-1/2-quart souffle dish; gently smooth top. Bake at 350 degrees on center rack for 50 to 55 minutes, until carrot mixture is puffed and set. Serve immediately.

Nutrition Information for Curried Carrot Souffle Servings Per Recipe: 6, Per Serving:4 g fiber, 510 mg sodium, 6 g pro., 29 g carb., 218 kcal cal., 6 g sat. fat, 10 g Fat, total, 126 mg chol.

Chocolate Pistachio Pudding Cake

1 Pkg Duncan Hines white cake mix
1 Pkg Pistachio Pudding mix (can be instant)
½ cup orange juice
½ cup water
½ cup vegetable oil
4 eggs
Optional ½ tsp vanilla
Optional 1/4 tsp almond extract
Optional Green food coloring
5 ½ oz. of Hersey Chocolate syrup

Blend all ingredients except 5 ½ oz. of Hersey Chocolate syrup or follow instructions on box
Mix 2 minutes with electric mixer (you should see a color and texture change)
Pour ½ the batter into a well-greased Bundt pan (I use vegetable oil, pour it in)

Add 5 ½ oz. of Hersey Chocolate syrup with the remaining half

Pour onto green batter – DO NOT MIX

Bake at 350 degrees for 50 to 60 minutes
Leave in pan to cool
Can frost, sprinkle with powdered sugar, or leave plain.

Millionaire Pie

Ingredients

2 prepared graham cracker pie crusts or 2 prepared Oreo dark chocolate pie crusts
1 can 15.25oz crushed pineapple, well drained
1 cup maraschino cherries drained & chopped
1 can Sweetened Condensed Milk 14 oz (Eagle Brand)
¼ cup lemon juice
13 ounces whipped topping (enough for two pies) plus extra for garnish if desired
Optional 1 cup sweetened flaked coconut
Optional 1/2 cup chopped pecans

Instructions

In a large bowl, combine crushed pineapple, maraschino cherries, sweetened condensed milk, and lemon juice.

Gently fold in whipped topping. Pour into crust.

Top with additional whipped topping and cherries if desired. Refrigerate 3 hours or overnight.

RACHEL'S SALSA DIP
(HELLMAN'S MAYONNAISE LABEL)

Mix all together and refrigerate
1 package Knorr Vegetable Recipe soup mix
1 cup mayonnaise (Boston uses Hellman's)
8 oz sour cream (this is 1 cup)
12 oz salsa - mild or hot (You may want to drain some juices before mixing)

GOURMET ONIONS
(HOME AND GARDENS 95¢ PAPER COOKBOOK 1966)

3 tablespoons butter or margarine
½ teaspoon monosodium glutamate
½ teaspoon sugar
¼ teaspoon salt
¼ teaspoon pepper
¼ cup sherry
10 – 12 small onions peeled cooked, drained
¼ cup shredded parmesan cheese

Melt butter in saucepan; stir in monosodium glutamate,

sugar, salt, pepper, and sherry. Add onions and heat quickly (about five minutes), stirring now and then. Turn into serving dish and sprinkle with cheese. Serves 6.

SAUSAGE-APPLE STUFFING
(GOOD HOUSEKEEPING)

1 pound pork-sausage meat
3 large apples, peeled and chopped
1 large onion chopped
1 cup chopped celery
4 cups fresh breadcrumbs
2 eggs
1 ½ teaspoons salt
1 teaspoon poultry seasoning

About 45 minutes before using:
In large saucepan over medium heat, cook sausage until browned, breaking pieces apart with a fork. With slotted spoon, remove sausage to medium bowl, set aside.
Pour all but ¼ cup drippings from saucepot. In drippings over medium heat, cook apples, onion and celery until celery is tender, about 10 minutes, stirring occasionally; remove from heat. Stir in reserved sausage and remaining ingredients; mix well. Makes enough stuffing for one 7– to -9 pound bird, about 6 1/4 cups.

Ham Hocks and Black Eyed Peas

Soak the dried peas overnight. Pour off the water. Season the ham hocks and peas with salt and pepper Boil in three quarts of water. Reduce to a simmer and cook, uncovered, 1 1/2 hours, or until peas and ham hocks are tender

YOU MAY EMAIL THE AUTHOR AT:

jaygeeheath@yahoo.com
jaygeeheath@gmail.com

Visit her website

http://www.jaygeeheath.com/

or look at her (seldom visited) Facebook page
https://www.facebook.com/jaygeeheath/

Find her books on Amazon and Kindle (Amazon being Amazon, type in the author's pen name jay gee heath to find her books.)

www.ingramcontent.com/pod-product-compliance
Lightning Source LLC
Chambersburg PA
CBHW040324300426
44112CB00021B/2874